MW01617304

About this book

What can reliably guide us in times of rapid change? Rachel Pollack and Johannes Fiebig focus on the daily Tarot card and simple magical practices and offer interpretations for each of the 78 Tarot cards which can easily be put into practice. In addition, they discuss perspectives reaching until 2024.

It has become common practice, since the time of the renowned Order of the Golden Dawn, to assign the Tarot cards to individual sections of the yearly cycle. These are known as the decans. This quality of time, which the Tarot cards also express (which, however, is largely unknown) is skillfully used by the authors.

About the Authors

Rachel Pollack is a poet, an award-winning novelist, a world authority on the modern interpretation of Tarot cards, and a Tarot card artist. Her novel *Godmother Night* won the 1997 World Fantasy Award.

Her thirty books include twelve books on the Tarot, including her opus magnum *Tarot Wisdom,* a summary of about 40 years of professional experience with the Tarot. She lives in New York's Hudson Valley. www.rachelpollack.com

Johannes Fiebig, born in Cologne in 1953, lives near Kiel, Germany. In 1989, he founded the Königsfurt Verlag (Koenigsfurt publications – together with Evelin Burger), which was sold to Königsfurt-Urania Verlag GmbH in 2007. He is one of the most successful authors on Tarot and a leading expert of the psychological interpretation of symbols and oracles. www.koenigsfurt-urania.com • www.tarotworld.com

Ernst Ott, Head of the School of Astrology, Karlsruhe/Germany. Founder member of the German Tarot Association (www.tarotverband.de). Numerous publications, including *Astrologie mit Tarot (Astrology with Tarot,* Tübingen 2005).
www.astrologieschule.org

Rachel Pollack — Johannes Fiebig

TAROT
for
Magical Times

Contributing article by

Ernst Ott

First edition
Krummwisch b. Kiel 2012

Copyright © 2011 by AGM Urania/Königsfurt-Urania Verlag GmbH
D-24796 Krummwisch / Germany
www.koenigsfurt-urania.com • www.tarotworld.com

Images Cover: Maya prophecy © frenta - Fotolia.com
Other images: s. List of References, p. 160
Tarot cards: Rider-Waite® Tarot, © 1971 US Games Systems,
Stamford/CT, USA.
Visconti-Tarot, © 1994 Lo Scarabeo, Torino/Italy.
Tarot der Marseille, © 2006 AGM AG Müller, Neuhausen/Switzerland.
Original Aleister Crowley Thoth-Tarot, © 1996, 2008 O.T.O.,
Austin/TX, USA, und AGM AG Müller, Neuhausen/Switzerland.

Cover design: Jessica Quistorff
Book design: Antje Betken and Stefan Hose
Typing: Gabriele Rose-Keszler
Translation and editing: Ulrich Magin
Printed in EU

ISBN 978-3-86826-537-8 (AGM Urania)
ISBN 978-1-57281-720-3 (U.S. Games Systems)

Contents

Foreword

Pluto in Capricorn

According to astrological standards—that is to say, across all the various astrological schools—**the years 2008 to 2024** represent a so-called phase in which Pluto is to be found in Capricorn. Pluto was the last planet to be discovered in modern times, in 1930. At the time of discovery, it was in Cancer. Today, after 80 and more years, Pluto has lost its status as one of the big planets. With its moons and star dust of the so-called "Edgeworth-Kuiper-Belt", it nevertheless marks the outmost dimension of our own solar system. This makes it symbolically a cipher, the embodiment of the unknown in the last, outer limits of our knowledge and consciousness.

The last phases when Pluto was in Capricorn (naturally, this was before its discovery) were the era of the Reformation (1516—1532) and the era of Enlightenment (1761—1778). The current phase will last from the end of 2008 until the beginning of 2024. The significance of 'Pluto in Capricorn' is that the basic tenets (of a society, even of a whole culture, but also of each individual) are being subjected to a process of change. This can lead to many things, such as the threat of a new form of fundamentalism or the revival of fanatical patterns of belief—but equally, in the end we may see the establishment of new, meaningful and sustainable fundamental values.

New Horizons

What is the characteristic of the time we live in? There are several accurate analyses of our era. To emphasize one from the English speaking world, we might mention the British historian Eric J. Hobsbawm and his book about the 20th century with the title 'The Age of Extremes'. And, as a representative for the German language, 'Der taumelnde Kontinent', by Philipp Blohm, a survey that illuminates our own time by reflecting the years from 1900 to 1914.

What is special, these studies suggest, what defines the 21st century, is the transformation of goals and horizons which are so ancient, so powerful, so far-reaching that they go back to the beginning of human civilization. This point of view is very well expressed by the British musician Sir Yehudi Menuhin: "If I had to sum up the twentieth century, I would say that it raised the greatest hopes ever conceived by humanity, and destroyed all illusions and ideals."

So we need not assume that "The end of the world is nigh", but rather recognize that "only" our old fundamental values, our horizons, have reached a certain goal. The coming years—and here we refer to the next stage until 2024—will challenge us to make our own contribution towards this renewal of value, to the exploration of new horizons.

Tarot—Tool of Change

Like Leonardo da Vinci's paintings, Michelangelo's sculptures and Albrecht Dürer's engravings, the Tarot cards are a part of humanity's heritage, they are a treasure of the West. And like the traditional fairy tales and myths, the Tarot cards have no individual authors but are a product of the Occident's *collective consciousness*.

The development of the **cultural good Tarot** is inseparably linked to the search of many generations of our modern era for new solutions and new horizons. Tarot is born in the Renaissance, an era of a new beginning after a mega-crisis (the plague in the Europe of the 14th century). The first book of interpretations for the Tarot cards was written by the priest and proponent of the Enlightenment, Antoine Court de Gébelin, in 1781, the year of the discovery of Uranus to shine the light of Enlightenment into "Le Monde Primitif", the uncivilized, original world. The modern boom, which is without comparison in the long history of Tarot, started with the Western Cultural Revolution around 1968, a time when many people were moved to look for new experiences and new forms of life.

This power of Tarot shows especially in the years of change of the 21st century. It even appears to us as if the images of the Tarot had developed in the course of the centuries to become riper and more powerful with each use, and as if their fruits, their unique value, would only come to full fruition in our present time.

Magical Times

What service and great opportunities the Tarot cards can offer is dealt with in the first part of this book in three chapters by three authors (pp. 11—48). Similar to a triptych, these essays show different explanations—which in fact complement one another—of the wonderful guidance that Tarot offers us: three approaches to survive the times of change and to use it creatively.

This book combines the Old and the New World (Europe and America), traditional and new perspectives of Tarot. It will be published in two languages on two continents at the same time—it is our contribution to learning from global experience.

We live at a remarkable time in the history of mankind. It is not the times as such that are magical—they become magical the moment we take the opportunities. When we awake the "magician" in us who knows who she / he is and what she / he does.

Rhinebeck / NY and Krummwisch / Kiel, 11.11.11
Rachel Pollack   Johannes Fiebig

Tarot
Tool of Change

It is the Moment, not the Date

Rachel Pollack

The Tarot came to life in Northern Italy at the beginning of the fifteenth century. For more than three hundred and fifty years it was known mostly as a game, the ancestor of Bridge, until suddenly, in 1781, its reputation and its use became changed forever. That was the year an occult scholar named Antoine Court de Gébelin published his conviction that the game known as *Les Tarots* (from the Italian *Tarocchi*) in fact originated in Ancient Egypt where mystical adepts and wise magicians used it as a disguise for their secret wisdom.

Since then people have been in love with this idea of the Tarot's hidden origin, along with its corollary, that the Tarot is a book of all knowledge, containing, for those trained to see it, the entire history and esoteric truth of the universe. As playing card historians have built up more and more details about early Tarot cards, some occultists have clung steadfastly to the idea of a secret origin, pointing out that the Tarot's structure and images fit so perfectly with mystical traditions, especially the complex system known as Kabbalah, that how could it possibly *not* carry a hidden text? Meanwhile, many historians have taken an equally strong stance, assuming that if they could prove the Tarot did *not* come from Egyptian magicians or mystical rabbis, then it must not mean anything at all, and all the occult "fantasies" and especially its use in divination will simply vanish.

But maybe both sides miss something very important about the Tarot's actual historical origin. The early fifteenth century was a time of intense significance for Europe, a moment of death and re-birth. Almost everything that had been stable for centuries seemed to come undone in one of the greatest epidemics in human history, bubonic plague, a Black Death that raged through most of the fourteenth century, killing a third of the population. And yet, out of the chaos and terror new life began to emerge—new translations of ancient texts, discoveries in art, the beginnings of experimental science, new formulations of mystical knowledge and magical systems—in short, the Renaissance, which began in exactly the time and place of the Tarot.

Playing cards, remarkably similar to the ones we use today, first came to Europe a certain time before, most likely brought back by soldiers from Crusader campaigns in—yes, Egypt. This was not the Tarot, however, just ordinary cards. "Tarocchi," to use its Italian name, began when someone thought to add an extra suit of "triumphi," or "trumps." These cards, with elaborate paintings of spiritual and secular images, such figures as a Pope, an Empress and Emperor, Death, an alchemist Hermit, and the resurrection of the dead, formed a powerful symbolic presentation, beyond their practical function in the game. Today we call them the "Major Arcana," (*arcana* is Latin for "secrets"), and refer to the four suits collectively as the "Minor Arcana."

People argue about exactly where the Tarot began, exactly when, exactly how, and for exactly what purpose. Such arguments may be missing the point of oracles and oracular devices. They are not linear, they do not belong to logical cause and effect of this-has-to-precede-that. *They belong to a moment, a time, but not a date.* Oracular devices—things we can use to generate "readings"—express qualities of spiritual meaning that can guide us in times of crisis, whether large or small, and it does not really matter if that in fact was their original design.

The Rider Deck

Consider the deck shown in this book, called the Rider for its original British publisher, or Rider-Waite-Smith for its two creators, designer Arthur Edward Waite and painter Pamela Colman Smith. Just as the original Tarocchi appeared in Italy at the end of a period of destruction, the Rider was published in 1910, just *before* what was possibly the greatest cataclysm in Europe since that fourteenth century Black Death. It is almost impossible for us today to grasp the devastation of World War I. Even though the death toll of the second war was much higher, it was the earlier one that shook Europe's deepest beliefs and assumptions about itself. And yet, just as with the Renaissance, the space created by the devastation led to surges of new life and thought, in such areas as physics and cosmology, art, literature, architecture, social movements for both good and evil.

The Rider deck comes from this period, it expresses that moment in large and small ways. Does it matter that it actually appeared just before the War, not after it? Oracles are of moments, not dates.

And now we too face catastrophic change and great spiritual openings. And so we turn to our culture's greatest oracle, the Tarot, which over the last hundred years has taken on even more meaning, more significance, as if all the books of interpretation, all the magical workings done with the cards, all thousands and thousands of readings, looked at in a certain way, can be said to have prepared the deck for its use right now, in this moment, as a guide through our own dangerous magical times.

When we think of Tarot readings we usually imagine questions of daily life—"When will I find a soulmate?" or "What kind of job should I seek?" or "What will happen if I sue my landlord?" The Tarot can help us with such issues (though sometimes not as specific as we might want, teaching us how we experience love rather than the time and place to meet a husband), but I'm not sure this is its real purpose. It's in times of crisis, when the world around us becomes filled with both danger and opportunity, that the Tarot really comes into its own. If we face such a time now, with predictions of catastrophe on all sides, from astrology to Christian apocalypse to environmental science, does it matter that the Tarot came into the world nearly six hundred years ago, designed for whatever purpose its creators consciously planned for it?

The Tarot's Chinese Cousin

We might grasp how the Tarot guides us if we look at its much older Chinese "cousin," the *I Ching* (The Book of Changes). The *Yi,* as translator Stephen Karcher calls it, developed over time, beginning some three thousand years ago, but it especially came together during periods of chaos and civil war. In such dangerous times both the powerful warlords and the ordinary people needed a guide to help them survive. They could not trust their own instincts and limited knowledge but had to know what in fact would work at any moment and what wouldn't. Should a leader move boldly forward, or would any forceful effort only lead to defeat and even disaster? There are times to act—the Chinese call the principle of action *yang*—and times to withdraw and be patient—*yin* is the Chinese term for the principle of stillness. In the Tarot we find these principles in the first two numbered cards of the Major Arcana (that is, after the Fool, card 0), the *Magician* and the *High Priestess.*

When someone casts the *I Ching* she creates a pattern called a hexagram, six lines that can be broken or unbroken. These describe the moment and what approach to the situation will be most useful. But while the diviner looks at the moment from the perspective of the person asking the question, the hexagram is understood to describe the quality of the much wider world in which the questioner plays a small role. The Tarot does something similar. It answers our immediate questions and needs but at the same time it looks beyond us to the web of energy and events that helps create our personal situation. In ordinary times we do not really need to look past our own needs, but in periods of catastrophe and rebirth seeing the wider moment can become absolutely essential.

The Tower and the Towers

A terrible demonstration of the Tarot's ability to respond to extraordinary world events occurred some ten years ago as I write this. From the end of August, 2001 through the first days of September, a number of Tarot readers around the world began to notice something strange. The card of the *Tower* seemed to show up in every reading. Whether people asked about love or family or finances, there was the *Tower*.

The more astute readers understood that even if the card meant something in each individual reading it was not really there for each of their clients. *Apparently, the Tarot was trying to send a message to the world through the individual readers.* Look at the card. Do you see the lightning struck tower in flames, the people leaping out of the windows? Now think back to September 11. Hijacked planes, not lightning, struck the World Trade Center, but the buildings were on fire, and for many who watched the nightmare unfold in real time on television the most awful sight was the people who leaped from the windows rather than stay and be burned.

The *Tower* card in all those readings "predicted" something terrible. But even if the readers had understood that these were not the usual *Tower* appearances, that the card was not about the individual clients, even if they somehow could have warned of something big about to happen—a psychic Tarot reader I know actually did predict the attacks, but from a dream not her cards—what could they have done with the information? Our current social structure does not pay any attention to messages gleaned from Tarot readings.

Suppose that were to change? Suppose one effect of a major shift in the world would be the return of oracles and diviners to a more prominent role? If we acknowledge the cards' power how can we best use them? There will be extraordinary situations, and maybe, just maybe, someone will create an internet clearing house for Tarot readers around the world to report unusual occurrences. And maybe people will start to notice such a site and begin to pay attention to it.

On a daily basis, however, maybe we should not worry so much about predictions but try to monitor what is happening, and most important, how we ourselves need to respond to it. So, we will continue to do personal readings but start to understand that our personal lives are part of something much bigger, and we need to recognize that if we are going to find our way.

Here is a follow-up to the story of the *Tower* card and 9/11. At the end of April, 2011, I and several hundred other Tarotists attended the Readers Studio conference in New York City, site of the 9/11 events. One of the participants happened to mention that the *Tower* card came up when she read the cards before traveling, and then again in every reading she did over the weekend. She understood it as a reference to a crisis in her personal life and did not think of it beyond that.

The conference ended on May 1, and most of us went home but this particular woman had a long trip and decided to stay an extra night. She went out to dinner that night (after another reading with the *Tower*) and when she returned she expected to go straight to her room, but when she entered the hotel she saw that President Obama was speaking on television. She walked up just as he was announcing the killing of Osama bin Laden.

It is the Moment, not the Date

That night, after seeing the news on the internet I decided to read the cards. No particular questions, just three cards to see what the Tarot wanted to say about this significant moment in our history. I decided to place the first card in the center and then one on each side as a commentary. Here is how they came out:

How should we interpret these cards? Many would say that the daring *Knight of Wands* action brought *Justice* through the *Death* of the leader of the Terrorists who destroyed the Twin Towers. But maybe the Tarot simply wanted us to look at whether that was in fact the case. Was Justice really done? Tarot cards don't always give us answers so much as make us look more closely at what is happening, and our own reactions. And maybe what we most need to recognize is that the cards can in fact reveal the power of large moments.

Prophecy and Rebirth

As I've worked on this book, re-interpreting the cards through the lens of crisis, change, and challenge. I've become more and more convinced that we can indeed see the deck as a kind of outline of the process of the world falling apart and then coming back together in a way that can release the past and bring a new world. This does not mean that we abandon the usual ways we understand the cards or do readings. It just means they work really well to look at them in the prophetic way. Am I suggesting the Tarot was designed with this in mind? Not at all. But then, it probably wasn't designed with Kabbalah in mind, either, and yet the Kabbalistic interpretation of the Tarot fits so perfectly it can be hard to believe that that was not its conscious purpose.

It is the Moment, not the Date

In this new approach I am suggesting, the Major Arcana represents the large outline of the fall of one world, one reality, and the spiritual liberation that will follow. The Minor Arcana, the four suits, show us different approaches to the hard task of surviving the fall, and building up a new society. To understand this better, let's first look at the deck's structure and some of the usual ways we see its meanings.

The Major Arcana

The Major Arcana consists of twenty-two cards, or as some people see it, twenty-one cards plus the *Fool* (in the game of Tarot the *Fool* is treated as apart from the others, and in old decks had no number at all, not even the 0 we find today). While some see each card as a distinct spiritual lesson separate from the others, most modern interpretations consider the cards as a sequence, beginning with the basic principles of the *Magician* and *High Priestess,* moving through such issues as relationship in *The Lovers* and fate in *The Wheel of Fortune,* and culminating in the high spiritual understanding of *The World.*

And the *Fool?* The *Fool* is the "hero" of the story, the Everyman who makes his way through the challenges of life to hopefully fulfill the lofty promise of the *World* card. And aren't we all fools, the best and the worst of us, stumbling along, trying to make it through life and figure out why we're here? A Tarot writer in the 60's named Eden Gray described the Major Arcana as "The Fool's Journey" and the name has stuck ever since.

To see the trump cards as prophecy requires only a small shift from our usual perspective. The *Fool* is still the journeyer but now he moves through a landscape of outer, cataclysmic events as much as the private inner journey to enlightenment. The final card, the *World,* still refers to individual awakening, but now it also, maybe primarily, means just what its title implies, the world itself radically changed, lifted from the debris of collapse, shown, among other cards, in the *Tower.*

People who look at the Major Arcana as a sequence often break it down into sections. I myself have tended to look at it as the *Fool* plus three rows of seven, cards 1-7. 8-14, and 15-21 arranged in three horizontal rows.

```
                  0
   1    2    3    4    5    6    7
   8    9   10   11   12   13   14
  15   16   17   18   19   20   21
```

Here, however, it seems to me to make sense to see the trumps in two halves.

```
  0    1    2    3    4    5    6    7    8    9   10
 11   12   13   14   15   16   17   18   19   20   21
```

Alternatively (and this is a developing process as we move into new territory for the world, and thus the Tarot), we can set the *Fool* aside as the journeyer, but also the *World,* as the "destination," and get the following:

```
                  0
   1    2    3    4    5    6    7    8    9   10
  11   12   13   14   15   16   17   18   19   20
                 21
```

In either approach we can look at the *Wheel of Fortune* as the culmination of the first half, and *Justice* as the launching of the second. This is because the *Wheel* treats life, including disasters, as just the mysteries of fate, something which we cannot understand and cannot change. *Justice,* however, challenges us to look deeper, to see the inner meaning, and to see how we ourselves help to create our own world.

It is the Moment, not the Date

The first half is the outer level of understanding, our usual way of moving through life. The second, starting with *Justice,* is the true prophecy, showing us such cards as *Death,* the *Devil,* the *Tower,* but then revealing the promise of the *Star,* and ultimately resurrection in *Judgment* and a new existence in the *World.*

Consider the *Wheel,* end of the first half, and the *World,* the final card (in English their names even sound alike).

Do you see how they resemble each other, the four figures in the corners, the circular wheel and the oval wreath of the dancer? In the *Wheel of Fortune,* however, everything is mysterious, symbolic, almost cartoon-like. We can see that it's filled with symbols, but without a reference book have no idea what they mean. Now look at the *World.* Everything there is fully painted, fully accessible, simple. This is not just the world restored, but raised up, with our own consciousness opened to experience everything that seemed outside of us in the first half. To get there, however, we have to make it through the dangers and challenges of *Death, The Devil, The Tower, The Moon,* and all the others.

We will understand these challenges better as we go through the individual cards. For each we also will look at some of their traditional "divinatory meanings," that is, how to understand them when they show up in readings. We will then add a recommended action to see how the card is speaking to us about the specific moment that we are facing, in that manner of the *I Ching.*

The Minor Arcana

The usual way to understand the Minor Arcana is to link the suits to the four "elements" of traditional astrology, Fire, Water, Air, and Earth. Each of these "rules" a certain area of life, and thus the suits also look at sets of experiences and ways of being in the world. There are different approaches but the Rider deck associates Wands with Fire, Cups with Water, Swords with Air, and Pentacles with Earth.

So what areas of life do these represent? Air/Wands deals with action, adventure, struggle, movement. Water/Cups shows us emotions, imagination, love, relationship. Air/Swords describes qualities of the mind, but especially conflict, sorrow, and difficult truths. Earth/Pentacles looks at such practical matters as work, money, nature, and physical conditions.

To look at the suits as paths to survive danger and restore a world we keep the basic meanings, only see them as part of large issues. Thus, each suit becomes a path, or way, for the world to move through "magical times."

Wands—the way of struggle. The cards show action, often heroic and highly individualist. The difficulty of working with others can limit Wands' effectiveness, so that the *Ten* shows a single figure burdened by responsibilities.

Cups—the way of the heart. Here we see people working together, sharing love. This very optimistic suit seems to fall apart in the middle numbers but then recovers at the end, so that the *Ten,* with its joyous family, gives us the most promising vision of all the suits.

Swords—the way of Sorrow. This suit is the most "difficult" but in its own way as necessary as the hopeful Cups, for it shows the mind struggling to come to terms with all that is lost. The frightening *Ten,* the image of a man dead with ten Swords in his back, actually contains hints of hope that if we truly let go of the past and the world's sufferings we can move on.

It is the Moment, not the Date

Pentacles—the way of the Earth. This is the practical suit, the image of people trying to build a new society on a day-to-day basis. Like the Cups, it begins optimistically, collapses in the middle, as if things are not so easy as they seemed, and then rebuilds itself to a stable prosperous situation in the *Ten.*

Court Cards

Of course, as well as Ace-Ten, each suit contains four Court cards, *Page, Knight, Queen,* and *King.* Though we list them with their suits, after the numbered cards, they form their own group, representing people rather than actions or events. But what people? Traditionally, readers have seen them as people in the questioner's life, and used physical characteristics to identify them. That is, *Kings* and *Queens* would represent men and women, *Knights* younger people, and *Pages* children or students. Wands Court cards meant people with blond hair and blue eyes, Cups light brown hair and hazel or brown eyes, Swords dark brown hair and brown eyes, and Pentacles black hair and black eyes. For this book it seems to make more sense to view the Court cards as ways to respond to crisis, danger, and opportunity.

Pages are youthful in their approach (though not necessarily physically young), optimistic, fresh.

Knights are heroic, dedicated, with a sense of service.

Queens hold the energy of the suit, its special power, and are aware of their responsibility on a spiritual level.

Kings exercise authority, they need to make decisions, not just for themselves but for their community.

Thus, if you get, say, the *Knight of Wands,* it suggests you move forward with daring, excitement, and a sense of adventure. If, on the other hand, you got the *Knight of Cups,* it would say to move much more slowly, turning your attention inward. In this way, the Court cards become more like a Book of Changes. That is, in one moment, the best response might be to express the qualities of the *Queen of Swords.* This would hold for a man as well as for a woman, for the cards are about ways of being not physical gender. In another moment, or in another view of the situation, the *King of Pentacles* might be what the person needs to act out. Nothing is fixed, for the glory of the Tarot is that we can always shuffle the deck and get a new perspective.

Interactions and Magical Tools

Though we look at each suit on its own, indeed each card on its own, true understanding comes when we see how they interact with each other (and of course, with the Major Arcana). For example, Wands and Pentacles look outwards, showing us action and physical conditions, including economic conditions. Cups and Swords, however, look inwards, examining the heart and the mind. We also can say the Wands and Swords are forceful and deal with conflict and heroic actions, while Cups and Pentacles concern themselves more with community. It's interesting to consider that if we look at where the happier, more successful cards seem to be, the deck appears to have a slight bias towards community and against individual heroism. This fact alone may give us a hint of the qualities we will need to create a new world.

Riding the Storm

Johannes Fiebig

Among those moments of cultural change that left their mark on the evolution of Tarot cards, I would like to count a very special era: the cultural revolution in the West—the time around 1968. "Imagination au pouvoir!" (let imagination rule!) was one of the slogans of the rebelling Parisian students in May 1968. The Hippie movement of the 1960s and the feminist movement of the West since the 1970s were the chief agents behind the mass circulation of the Tarot.

It started with the Hippies

All which we now take for granted in Tarot only originated in and around 1968: millions of people all over the world who started to lay the cards (for themselves); hundred, now even thousands of different deck designs, most of all Rider Waite Deck and the Crowley Deck, both of which were first printed in this time, as f.e. the Crowley Tarot. The Rider Waite Tarot also saw its first mass printings then. The many books with interpretations, movies, novels, theatrical or musical pieces, giftware, bedclothes or socks, all with motifs taken from the Tarot—were neither known in the Renaissance nor in the esoteric circles of the 19th century.

"Between mystical rubbish and an intellect opposed to dreaming, Tarot now playfully addresses intuition. Its images concentrate the philosophical and religious experience of many eras and an esoteric and occult tradition," as ZEIT, one of the big European weeklies, explained in 1984, at a time where it was hardly possible not to notice the Tarot boom, in a page-long article. This was further proof that Tarot had finally reached the public and cultural mainstream.

Tarot is the ideal tool, the perfect mirror in a time when many people are searching for identity and reliable values, for new knowledge and for the path to a happier or more prosperous life and love. This power of the Tarot is evident also—and outstandingly—in the years of change of the 21st century.

Passion for Learning

As all symbolic languages and oracles, Tarot is of special help if we reach dead ends with all other means, when we are at our wits' end.

We draw one or several cards; and their symbols (or those of dreams, fantasy journeys, consulting the pendulum, of sayings or other messages)—these words and symbols show us paths. These we test, and by becoming active and opening up for new experiences, we will discover new opportunities in our real life.

This works especially well when the cards help us by letting us discover—in them and through them—really new aspects of life. One of the cards which can teach us most, which is a powerful advisor—is the card *The Tower*.

It was neither planned, nor did we talk about this in advance, that all three contributors to this volume (Rachel, Ernst and I) would give the *Tower* a central importance in this book about "Tarot as Companion in Change." Yet it is no accident: *The Tower* is an image of the highest energies we know. And without gaining expertise in dealing with this *high energy* it appears almost impossible to pass through this crisis and change with fortune and a good ending.

Look—don't run away

Rachel, who lives near New York City, tells how 9/11 felt for her and many other Tarotists (cf. pp 15-17). I live in the north of Germany, in old Europe. However, this Tuesday in September 2001, I spent in Tuscany, Italy, leading a Tarot workshop for a tour operator from Southern Germany. Our intention was to enjoy Tarot and Tuscany for a week with sense and all senses.

In precisely this week we heard the news about the attacks in New York City and Washington. The different people in our group reacted differently. Some wanted to cancel their stay and return home as soon as possible. Others tried hard to ignore the news and just to go on. Other again felt confused—shocked, yet uncertain what to.

We postponed any decision, meditated and went for a hike. We also thought hard about the card *The Tower* as represented in different decks.

"The Tower" in the Tarot of Marseilles, the Rider-Waite-Smith deck, and the Crowley deck (left to right)

The Eye of the Tiger

We see a tower, a thunderbolt hitting it, fire, and a crown falling on one side or standing, and two figures falling and/or flying. Interestingly, we do neither see the very moment they jump or are thrown out, nor the moment they land or crash on the ground. We are concerned here with the time *in between*—between heaven and earth, the realm of the angels, of which Shakespeare said, "There are more things in heaven and earth, than are dreamt of in your philosophy."

We discussed that in our group. None of the participants would have had the idea to select this as their favorite card. Again and again, the current events in the US showed in sudden tears and in emotions of helplessness: *In one instance, all seemed without sense.*

Some in that night dreamt of the bomb attack nights of WWII. (which they had not experienced themselves, but vividly recalled from stories told).

Others, however, had—independent of the recent events—positive associations to the topic *Tower*: Lighthouses help in difficult navigation, they enable people to navigate and steer a course in the first place. Some people enjoy towers: high divers at the pool or parachutists who love to literally "jump out of the clouds." A psychologist added that jumping, falling, and flying are not only related to fear, but also to lust and fun in real life as well as in dreams. And I know that card XVI in the *Tarot de Marseille* has always been called *La maison dieu*, the *House of God* or *God as Homeland!* Not all of this means destruction or crash.

Two contrasting Archetypes

The following day—Wednesday, September 12—all participants decided to stay. We continued our daily meditation, and the workshop went on with a heightened awareness. We now had the topic of archetypes on our agenda. It stood to reason that we had a close look at *The Tower.*

This card actually reflects two archetypes. One the one hand, this is the *Tower of Babel*, and on the other, the event of *Pentecost*.

The Tower of Babel was an expression of human hubris (and, as a tower also always is a phallic symbol, we may add: an expression of *male* hubris). This led to the destruction of the tower. The builders were thrown back to earth, and their attempt resulted in the *Babylonian confusion of languages*. Since that event, the peoples of this earth no longer understand each other!

The event of Pentecost, to the contrary, is just the opposite: it lifts this confusion of languages and barriers to understanding. Christ's disciples met in one place, as narrated in the Acts of the Apostles, and they were all filled with the Holy Ghost, and began to speak with other tongues, and were understood by all in their mother tongue!

The event of Pentecost signifies the overcoming of language barriers, and in the bottom line an end to barriers of understanding of all kinds.

The Descent of the Holy Spirit is shown in the Rider-Waite image as yellow drops of fire which recall the Biblical tongues of fire. The Crowley deck depicts the Holy Spirit directly in the form of a white dove with a palm leaf. The first person to actually connected *The Tower* to Pentecost in mind was—as far as I know—Papus, one of the past masters of esoteric Tarot interpretation.[1]

The "Tower" stands for High Energies

For our group in Tuscany the power of the archetypes was almost tangible. Archetypes represent patterns of behavior of the soul which may develop great force. This does sound abstract most of the times, but in our case needs not much explanation. The *Twin*

1 In his book "Tarot des Bohémiens", published in 1888 in Paris. "Bohémiens" means gypsies, but it also refers to "bohèmes", the Parisian "Hippies" of the 19th century.

Towers in Manhattan had actually been destroyed because of their symbolic importance.

High energies we experience involuntarily are, in the worst case, *violence*; and forceful, unreasonable demands and violations can even today rob us our speech and, as in Babylon, language and understanding!

The most positive use of the highest energies, however, is *love*. With love, we can still experience our own Pentecost each day. Even today it is possible to overcome barriers of language and understanding in the spirit of love. This is true, for example, if you fall in love in a foreign country: love then enables you to step over the limitations of language. Yet the same is true in our own country, as every individual, in a sense, has his or her own language. The power of love enables us to leave our *ivory tower*, to unmask, to no longer hide behind walls of objections and false pretenses, but to open ourselves and let ourselves fall, to make our contribution.

We experienced this power to break crusts, to show one's real face to oneself and others, in the remaining days of this week. It turned this workshop into one of the liveliest, most moving and effective that I have ever had.

... and Peaks

The following day—Thursday, September 13—we visited the famous Tarot Garden by Niki de St. Phalle. It includes a more than 13 feet high statue representing the Tower hit by a thunderbolt. In the gigantic interior of the figure of the *Empress* in the Tarot Garden we laid out the cards. This, again, was an unforgettable experience.

In the cards we picked, *The Tower* didn't show up too often. Yet we looked at it again and again in different representations. We may interpret this image of the Waite Tarot as a tower hit by lightning, and people being thrown off it. But this would be the involuntarily, violent version.

But we may interpret the image as two persons who have dared to drop off, who have left their aloofness, their petrification, their isolation, and their egoism. In real life, they find their equivalent in intensified life situations that "have reached a point," in which someone, for example, quits a job because he or she can't bear it any longer, without having a new job offer. The same is true for relationships, when we leave a relationship that has become a tower-like prison, which has led to a hardening and a cutoff from the world. Divorce or separation then release enormous energies.

The same is true in the case of a new care and opening for a person we've not known before! "To meet a person at his center is to pass through a revolution yourself," Osho said, and this is also shown by the image. Indeed, the Order of the Golden Dawn, the Rosicrucian group who was very influential in the history of Tarot, called this card, among other interpretations, "Revolution."

Last, but not least, the *Tower* is not only a phallic symbol, but, of course, with its fireworks and its rain of fire, it also represents an image of orgasm in the concrete and figurative sense. It is an image of peaks and high energies.

In this sense we may look at the card. *First*, the people risk jumping off, they break free from isolated and petrified conditions, and this jump into the unknown, this openness for the other and the new, releases huge amounts of life energies which are symbolized by the lightning flash in the picture.

Breathe deeply

As we returned to our country hotel from the Tarot Garden, inspired and grounded, and switched on our TV sets we couldn't fail but notice that large sectors of public life were filled with certain hysteria a few days after 9/11. People who had been opposed to war suddenly became advocates, liberals waived basic rights, gentle intellectuals called for a strong state, and much more.

Riding the Storm

One of our group members noticed that there are two destructive 9/11's in American history. While everybody was discussing September 11, 2001, and the attacks especially in New York City, there had also been a September 11, 1973—exactly 28 years before—when the presidential palace of the democratically elected government of Salvador Allende in Chile was attacked and he ousted by bombs with the support by parts of the US Secret Service. No government agency talked about that, not then, in the year 2001, not in any of the services commemorating 9/11 in later years. Hysteria knows no reflection, and it has no memory.

Riders on the storm

This song of the American group The Doors accompanied the final rounds of our workshop.

Into this world we're "thrown"—that was one of the key ideas of existentialism, the philosophy of the 1950s. If we want to realize that, we need leave our shell and risk an own design, an own design for a living. This is what the hippies had learned from the existentialists, and had put into practice. Tarot is about this heritage of the generation that preceded us in the card *The Tower*, but generally through the Tarot boom that started in this time.

Whoever dares an own design for a living will become a "Rider on the storm." To fashion this ride is love and work, working for knowledge, "building relationships": whether in a relationship to others or in relation to oneself. It is love and work to unmask, to destroy the backdrop of alleged constraints and unused opportunities: "Let us be aware of the present, the moment," I told the participants at the farewell. "Let us learn to work with all energies! We are better protected against violence, hysteria, and unreasonable demands of any kind the more conscious we are dealing with the 'higher energies.' Let us now return home, and may we continue to 'ride the tiger.'"

New Life Blossoms In The Ruins

"Pluto in Capricorn", 2008 – 2024

Ernst Ott, astrologer

The Tower

The Star

Judgment

It is a part of the mystery of this first card—The Tower—that we often react emotionally to it, with horror, fear or sympathy. One of the gifts of the sign of Capricorn, however, is the ability for sober reflection. With it, we see what a tower aims at. What causes people to live in a tower? Perhaps they have faced a negative and extreme situation. Towers can be prisons. The people, then, would have been robbed of their freedom. And those who go to live in a tower on their own free will must have been threatened, most likely by a state of war. The tower forms a place of relative security in a time of great anxiety. Let us have a second look: one must feel pretty unsecure to voluntarily confine one's space of living to a square of 12 by 12 ft. with only arrow loops to let the light in. With this in mind, anxiety better describes the state before the thunderbolt hit, when the world only seemed to be secure. The situation the people face may be new and unfamiliar, but not actually horrible.

We put a sober question: How has life changed, now that the people are outside of the tower? If they had been prisoners, they are liberated now. If they were warlords in their fortress, they are now also in the fresh air. Their security has gone to pieces. As this was caused by a thunderbolt, and not by an enemy bomb or cannon ball, they now may either relax and enjoy the fresh air or plan new strategies or decide to rebuild the topmost floor.

First Phase: Destruction of Walls

Pluto in Capricorn first of all symbolizes the breakdown of the old order. In the sphere of society, this concerns instable organizations, structures, and states; in the personal realm, dogmas, fears, and die-hard habits, possibly even incrusted affairs and relationships. Those who have felt secure in them will possibly see this security crash.

Capricorn tends to build up security at the cost of harsh consequences. At first, this does not contradict Pluto's "intentions." Yet Pluto is the necessary corrective in cases where the strive toward security endangers life. Then you need to discern between security and security. All concepts of security which protect and allow life make sense. However, all security measures based on fear are questionable. They limit and prevent life. In mythological terms, this is equal to the difference between the nurturing Saturn of the Golden Age and the Saturn who eats his own children.

Exercise: True and False Security

1. **Note down all that gives you security,** just as it comes to mind: fellow humans, financial resources, mental concepts, objects, places etc.

2. **Now calculate the cost you have** to pay to possess this security at each point. This cost may either be material or mental. Some of your fellow humans, for example, might make you feel secure, yet they demand your good will etc. Compare cost and profit.

3. **Finally, take stock:**

   For which security do you pay a fair price, one you happily spend?

   Which security, in the long term, limits you and robs you of your joy in life, or limits your space for movement? Do you really need it?

If we encounter useless, life-preventing securities during this analysis of profit and loss in Capricorn, we can either expect a thunderbolt very soon, which overthrows seemingly secure walls—or remove the stones on our own. Many people hesitate or remain passive, as the removal of stones means work. By that, they unconsciously choose variant one. They let fate do all the work. And when the thunderbolt has finally hit, they accuse fate for ignoring them and not politely asking in advance what kind of thunderbolt they would prefer.

The breakdown of the old order may thus be experienced in different ways:

    1st variant: It will not be understood as horrible or negative, as one was unaware before how limiting the old order had been or because one had suppressed it. The breakdown of the walls is seen as something fateful.

Pluto in Capricorn

In this case, soon after the walls have collapsed, the walled-in anxieties show. The person concerned will misidentify this and think: this act of god—in our picture, the thunderbolt hitting the tower—caused my fears. Actually, this is not the case, as the tower was erected to wall in these fears. Living certainly was limited, but relatively safe. The fears were just ignored. Now they come into the open, and they are the same old fears. In the next phase their history should be investigated. How and when did they originate? How did I immobilize them or wall them in? Which advantages and disadvantages did the suppression have?

2nd variant: The breakdown of the old order is longed for as a hope. The Tarot card with the tower hit by lightning can also be interpreted as liberation from prison. When you sit in a prison cell, all you want is freedom. When lightning hits, it doesn't matter whether you escape comfortably on a flight of stairs or fall through a window—the important thing is becoming free. There are many people in the world who are wrongly imprisoned and hope for the old order to break down.

There are situations in life in which we—without actually being imprisoned—feel as if we were in prison. In some cases, liberation could happen under Pluto in Capricorn by "coincidentally" destroying those coercive forces which hindered us or by removing those people who were our prison guards.

3rd variant: Another option to react to the first phase of Pluto in Capricorn is the following: the crash of the old security which already was a thing of the past is voluntarily brought about. A clear understanding of its true character leads us to self-liberation. The picture of the tower always reminds me of the famous saying by Kant that "enlightenment is man's emergence from his self-incurred immaturity."[2] A door, leaving

2 Immanuel Kant, beginning of the tractate WAS IST AUFKLÄRUNG?, Hamburg 1999.

New Life Blossoms In The Ruins

a state which does not make you free. At least in retrospective we may understand that this state was of our own design. External influences caused it, but our own, still limited spirit saw no other way to bear the prison. Astrology is a tested means for searching for still undiscovered emergency exits. It can show people new possibilities and enable them to choose more freely.

Second Phase: New life blossoms in the ruins

There is a time when each and every wound has healed. Whether this comforts you depends on how you look at things. The objective problem with this is that blooming cannot be willed but takes its time. The whole phase lasts 16 years, and those who are personally affected by a Pluto transit have to wait several months, even years, depending on whether you count with a longer or shorter orbis. What you now need is the quality of patience of Capricorn.

Basically, in this middle phase, we are talking about a state in which you in fact can change nothing about the circumstances. I recommend you simply use this time to work with your inner mental attitude. Despite this, it can become quite uncomfortable that you cannot do anything wrong or right on the level of action, that you cannot control anything at this time. People who, by their character, easily access the will-power of the sign of Capricorn or who would love to control by Pluto, will feel especially powerless. They have

Star, Tarot de Marseille

Pluto in Capricorn

a hard time suffering that time is the agent of action, that fate acts, that nature acts, but not they. We may regret that, but the solution lies in both symbols: positive Pluto can integrate magical powers which are larger than individual personalities. Positive Capricorn can enable you to reach wise insights into the passage of time. The Greek god Kronos-Staturn is also Chronos, the lord of time. Both solutions require a certain mental effort, so this phase harbors the danger of the outer stillness paralyzing us. We become passive, feel victimized.

Perhaps some people should indeed learn to accept help. This requires inner strength most of all. The aim of all help, that of astrology especially, lies in revitalizing the initiative of those concerned.

In contrast, others are not afraid to accept help, but they are not offered any. What is offered seems too little to them. They feel life treats them unfair. It is not easy for them to break free from their role as victim. Because being a victim guarantees sympathy and empathy. Our society takes victims seriously—at least in the face it shows to the public. All that, reinforced by our long established culture of moaning, makes it difficult for those concerned to start their initiative, because being a victim guarantees enough substitute tender loving care, also, you must never feel guilty for what you are. People cultivate a secret defiance against life and believe that the world owes them everything. They feel they have every right to remain passive and expect solutions from the outside.

There can be no question that society and those who cause suffering have a responsibility for their victims. But astrology (and the Tarot, as well) should return some of the initiative to the victims. How small whatever our own part is of the whole: we may use this little thought. We alone are responsible for our mental concepts, our thoughts and feelings. And we are completely free to change them.

New Life Blossoms In The Ruins

Our contribution to the second phase, then, consists in becoming active internally, and in cultivating a sedate hope externally: I trust in nature and in the healing power of time.

Rethinking also includes the capacity to perceive freshly. In this phase we must learn so see again. Just imagine you were one of the two persons who are thrown out of the tower. Although they are free, they are still seeing everything through the lens of the tower. Now we imagine that, just on the horizon, a second group of people with a flag appears. Our two people will react with fear. In the last few years, they have tried not to look out of the arrow loops in order not to see the horrible enemies. They were always hoping that their walls were strong enough. Their task now is to learn to see and observe again: In case the approaching group of people actually carries a war banner and is armed with sticks, it were useful to recognize that as soon as possible and to react in an adequate way. Their protective walls are gone, and anxiously waiting will not help. They might get beaten—but they just might win. This would not have been possible inside the tower. It can only be done when you are outside, assess what is real, and act.

Judgment, Tarot de Marseille

You could tell this story with a negative ending: both people just do not want to learn to see again. They just fuzzily discern people and a flag, sit down on the turf beside the tower's ruin, and are convinced that heavily armed enemies are soon going to defeat them. After some time, all the noise ceases, and they open their eyes again. Had they not closed their eyes, they would have seen words on the banner: "We are going to celebrate! Join us!" The only arms the unknown people were carrying were musical instruments and bottles of sparkling wine. Fear is not the best counselor. We may now inform the two that the foreigners had only good intentions. But would they believe us?

Pluto in Capricorn

Their former arrow loop focus will see only enemies. The old fear blinds them to new realities.

Third Phase: Resurrection of all that is buried

In any case, the result of this process is that something has become visible and manifest which up to now was deep in the shadows. What formerly was hidden below ground is now illuminated by the light.

There is no guarantee that it will be something nice. It could well be the return of something suppressed, a resurrection of characters of the past who are not welcome. Before we resign and mourn our fate, we might do well to remember what we have learned: first of all, even if a monster has been brought to light, it will be far easier to fight it in the light of day than in the dark of night. Second, it might be less of a monster than it seemed to be. The processes of Pluto so far have, we hope, made us so insecure that our fixed terms for what is good and what is bad have been shaken. Light and darkness are not easily divided, they just merge. This is no comfortable state, but it has its advantages when it comes to discovering the good parts of the so-called bad or the many shades of color that exist between black and white.

But what can we do when our resurrected figures are by far uglier than those in the picture? If suddenly characters, behavioral patterns and drives appear which we so far held to be our dark sides and which we tried to arrest in a dark corner of our soul? That's too bad! This would mean that the expected liberation of the prisoners sets free quite a few creatures whom we'd rather not meet. It's a shame, but we cannot just tell our dark sides that we are sorry and do not know them. In such a case we need to step back! We have returned to phase one, we are still afraid of lightning and change. We get the opportunity for a repeat performance of the second phase to learn rethinking. Again, we need to look at events without prejudice until we can see the flowers that blossom in the ruins.

Let me add some practical advice: Usually, it is impossible for you to tame your darker sides; you can only hide them. If this—as we just have discussed—is not possible, you can only learn to love them. Now that they have stepped out into the limelight, we need to observe them carefully and full of interest until we find that they a not as dark as we thought. Happily, we take them for a walk. There is no foundation for our assumption that this will lead to a loss of friends, or will make us lonely. We might lose a few "holier than thou" friends, but the rest will instinctively feel that dealing with us has become more exiting and interesting. The way we behave now will make our friends recall their own darker sides.

Based on solution oriented astrology, we will concentrate on the positive potential of this resurrection of all that was buried in the following. The figures on the picture directly suggest the possibility of support by our ancestors. If you believe that our forefathers are not just dead and gone and no longer have any power, but can be asked for help, this is the best time to awaken these resources and to make use of them.

But even those who do not believe in our ancestors' support may strive for a strengthening in a psychological sense by dissolving negative and emotionally draining memories while, on the other side, honoring strengthening memories of good experiences with the ancestors, and using them. Things that were wrongly programmed in the past (Capricorn) may be re-programmed now (Pluto).

It might be instructive to analyze the horoscopes of siblings, parents, or grandparents. We will discover inherited patterns, clusters in the occupation of a certain zodiacal sign, or even the same zodiacal degree or something similar. This will make clear that we are not alone, and not the first ones to have that special problem!

Pluto in Capricorn

Even if we discover a difficult family script (in former times, this was called a curse jinxing a clan), we do no longer need to be the blind victim of this unconscious, collective mechanisms. I am convinced that when we live this family aspect more freely and constructively than in our past, we will not only help ourselves, but our family as well.

Part of the possible resurrection of previously unseen aspects is Pluto's correlation to magic. Defining the term more loosely, it simply means: powerfully changing something, starting something, achieving something, and this by using irrational forces. What would never work under the condition of cause and effect may happen nevertheless. Even such logical devices as machines have their irrational aspect, life even more so. These 16 years offer us the opportunity to increasingly use holistic arts. I am thinking about methods of life or economic management which make full use of the forces of the unconsciousness, methods which cannot completely be rationally explained, but simply work, like spiritual healing, homeopathy, family constellation, astrology, rituals, dream interpretation, and much more.

We are here dealing with a double resurrection, because, at one hand, these methods draw on the hidden treasures of the unconscious, on the other hand they are very old and have long been declared dead by Enlightenment, and now are happily reborn. As we all know, there's life in the old dog yet. Perhaps, in the past and in modern times, astrology has more often been pronounced dead than any other technique. It is certainly not by chance that it is one of the few systems which have constantly been reborn and in that way survived intact over millennia. This Plutonic event is comparable to the well-known fact that a deep crisis survived or danger of death makes those hit by them only stronger. They leave a kind of death behind; therefore, they fear it less than others. This makes them almost immortal.

New Life Blossoms In The Ruins

The Shadow Topic in the Horoscope

Pluto in Capricorn aids a resurrection of the shadow in the horoscope. In our school, we assume that the so-called shadow topics—this term is borrowed from Jungian depth psychology—often have a fearful connotation, yet basically indicate a kind of giftedness. In my many years of practical interpretation work it stood the test of time to use the hypothesis that one's strongest shadow also is one's strongest talent. It contains far more intensity and force for survival than most of the already known talents. It carries more energy than the lighter natural talents that show early and seldom cause problems.

To discover hidden talents under Pluto in Capricorn could mean

- to accept and cultivate unused abilities
- to train new behavior in the creative sector
- to activate live dreams that you have not yet lived
- to reawaken lost professional plans
- to take seriously again forgotten biographic visions
- to re-evaluate childhood dreams

In general, we need to disgorge our swallowed children, and to talk to them. Pluto aids us at this moment and gives us enormous power. Therefore, it makes sense to put down the "impossible"-signs at certain places and replace them by "possibly possible"-signs. To look at such a sign will encourage our own courage.

In the following, you find a further interpretation of the three phases as a task to do. It will be formulated in the form of a job instruction sheet. This enables us to change the role of the observer with that of the actor. Those words we have used till now do not address your individual responsibility. "Destruction of walls," as we have called the first phase up until now, can be understood in an active sense. I courageously destroy what is no longer needed. But it can also be read as an expectation at fate. The second phase,

Pluto in Capricorn

"new life blossoms in the ruins" sounds quite a bit like a promise of happiness to which one need not contribute anything. The third sentence is similar. Therefore, I give three alternative titles which simply express what you could do yourself.

Destroying Fears

For a start, we should tear down the walls of fear that handicap us. We can unmask false security as a prison and break free to reach more meaningful security on a new level. We have the opportunity to clear away the rubbish from our past.

The most difficult part will be to recognize, in the first place, that we have been governed by fears in some sectors. Limiting conditions are partly the result of external influences. But our attitude up to now, that we just can do nothing about it, was dictated by fear. We have to question it. We have never entertained certain variants of behavior because we thought something horrible might result. The truth of this suspicion must be thoroughly tested. Thoroughly and without emotion. With the objectivity of a positive Capricorn. Destruction of fears must not always be a dramatic act. Assiduous and good self-analysis will certainly work.

For some limiting conditions we will find that we ourselves have walled us in. This makes it easier to dismiss our own fears now because we opt for a different security strategy in our future.

I warn again that in tearing down we should be clever. As soon as the walls collapse, they will release the fears that were caught inside! You now need to withstand the feeling that all has turned for the worse. This would mean to misidentify cause and effect. Those fears were constantly present in the former phase of suppression. Their subliminal effect was even stronger as these fears masked a reason. So this fear emerging now is nothing new! It is a thing of our past. As the walls are torn down, it comes up again, only to disappear.

Take your Time!

Part of the symbolism of Capricorn and Saturn is Chronos, the lord of almighty and all-changing time. As courageously as we must act in phases one and three—we must let time take effect in the space between. Time heals all wounds. But it takes more time if we impatiently thresh around and let it not do its work.

In this time between, we have the opportunity to change our attitudes. This time can be used for reflection. If we are honest to ourselves: there is little that could be more exciting than dealing with ourselves.

If we re-evaluate and gain new perspectives on what we held to be good or bad, we create valuable material for building a better future. This needs some practice. Those who use their time for reflecting and loving self-education will not find it boring to wait for the new bloom.

Beside the serious work to discover in which sectors we unconsciously see through a lens of fear, and the subsequent phase of practice to change the fear, beside all these focused actions it might be valuable to simply look out of the window like a child, and concentrate on all that is new and passes by. Opportunities need to be recognized, first of all. As we do not yet know in which form they will appear, we should approach the window without any fixed intention. The window no longer is an arrow loop, we can look freely. As we are not after anything definite in this phase, we should put a cushion on the window sill, bide our time, and just be curious.

Awaken Shadows

He we should do all humanely possible to integrate the shadow. All that was foreign to us might become a part of us. I do not intend to judge whether cultural diversity is a sociologically sound concept, but when we deal with our inner self, we have no choice: we need to integrate the foreign, because we cannot call for the aliens' police

to deport it. No matter how alien our inner Pluto may appear to us, no matter how much he smells of garlic or displays undemocratic behavior: it is a part of ourselves.

There's no need to make things difficult. We must not become saints in the course of 16 years and be completely devoid of shadows. If we simply accept that fact that there still is a piece of Neanderthal man in us, this means a giant step forward compared to the state of fear and suppression of the former inhabitants of the tower. And if we start talking to him, we have made great progress. By the way, Neanderthal man even might be a talent. As a bodyguard, he might be an asset to over-adapted people who remain calm and polite even in confrontations with rowdies.

We have already explained how astrology can be used to better define hidden talents, and where to look for them.

Even positive talents can, if released for the first time after years of negligence, appear a bit shadowy. They cannot show their best side from the beginning. Perhaps we address our potential talent, "I know I haven't really pampered you in the past. But I welcome you in the future, no matter how you behave. We will have a closed season for a year while you make your home in my inner apartment-sharing community."

Finally, it needs to be stressed once more that events will not always take place in the order of these three phases, other orders are possible, or one phase might be more emphasized than the rest. Sometimes we may go through all three steps several times, even concerning the same topic. Life uses repetition, and there always is a second chance.

History reloaded

"There are further reasons to deal with this symbolic resurrection of the ancestors under Pluto in Capricorn. By studying their horoscopes and researching the family's history, we learn things about our forefathers which we didn't know before. This is a basic (Capricorn correlation) gain that gives us courage on our own way. We suddenly learn of a member of our family who hat a life design similar to our own. Another of our ancestors shared similar values to our own. It is even possible that we feel closer to a link in this chain than to our own parents. Suddenly, we feel less alone. It is said that we can't change the past. I do not believe this, as we at least can rethink it. I know many people who gained a completely new outlook to life through a Plutonic rethinking of the past. Formerly, they thought that everything was bad, now they also find many beautiful and valuable things in their childhood. Formerly, they found it easier to forget. Today they love to remember or at least accept their own life history." (Ernst Ott)

Readings and practical advices

Rachel Pollack

Oracular systems give us a method to reach beyond our limited information—beyond any human information, really—to find out what is going on in our world and what we need to do, what we *can* do. Oracles are a special kind of search engines—they start, where Google ends.

The process is called *divin*ation, because we learn to see the way the gods might see, perceiving the inner truth of the present and the possibilities of the future. In times of great upheaval the Tarot, like its older cousin, the *I Ching*, guides us by showing us our own place in the greater world. This larger context is implied in every Tarot reading, whether we look for it or not, even the most personal or trivial readings. Because it captures the greater framework the Tarot can help us navigate through a drastic period in the world. The spreads (patterns for laying out the cards) given in this book will address ourselves and our place in the world around us.

How To Do It

The basic technique of reading Tarot cards is really quite simple. Some find it valuable to do it in a ritual manner, lighting candles, setting out magical objects, holding hands with the "querent" (the one seeking the reading), closing the eyes and breathing deeply before beginning, even saying a prayer. But really the basic process does not change, and all you need is three things: a querent, a reader, and a pack of Tarot cards. If you are reading for yourself, then the querent and the reader are the same person, but the process is the same.

The querent asks a question, sometimes more than one, or states an area of concern. For example, she or he might say "Will I find love after my divorce?" or "I want to look at my love life." And they might add "I also want to know whether I have a future in my current job." The querent then shuffles the deck—face down, so they cannot see which card is which—and gives it back to the reader. The reader then turns over the cards, usually in a set pattern known as a "spread." Many readers will interpret the cards one at a time, some turn them over all at once, and speak to the entire pattern. Most do a combination, that is, they speak about each card but at the end try to tie everything together.

You will notice above that for each card we have given a "Reversed" set of meanings along with the basic set, called "Divinatory meanings (see p. 60)." Reversed means that they person shuffled them in such a way so that some cards come out upside down.

Not everyone reads reversed cards (so Johannes, see pp. 100). They find that the card right side up contains all its possibilities—positives and negatives—so why have a separate set of meanings? Sometimes, however, the particular meanings of the card reversed are just what we need to know.

Spreads

One Card

The simplest spread is one card. What do I need to know? Or, what is this moment?

Many people actually do this, pull one card a day, especially as a method to learn the cards. They find that the more dire cards, such as the *Devil* or the *Ten of Swords,* become less scary when they know it's only for one day. Here, however, we are looking at one card readings in a slightly different way. If our personal lives, and even more, the world itself, is in a long crisis then checking the cards each day, as a way to guide us, can be very helpful, maybe even crucial to our very survival.

Here's an example, done just as I would do an actual reading. I shuffle the cards and get the *Hierophant.*

In this moment tradition and spiritual authority are uppermost. Either we ourselves can exercise authority, especially in the service of others, or we must look to others who can guide us. Of course, it makes sense I would get this card right now—after all, I'm writing about Tarot cards! But as a way to chart through a crisis, the *Hierophant* points to the power of spiritual structures—churches, temples, doctrines, all that the card signifies.

Two Cards

Asking "What is this moment" seems to call for a second card. "How should I respond to it?" So, I reach into the deck again, and I get

   1. What is the moment? *Hierophant*
   2. How should I respond to it? *Moon*

In this moment of Hierophantic tradition I need to be aware, to *respond*, with a sense of mystery, of the deep levels of instinct. Without the *Moon* the *Hierophant* becomes dry, a set of rules and doctrines.

Responding with the *Moon* brings the *Hierophant* to life as a true spiritual teaching. (Again, this was a genuine reading, done for this passage.)

Three Cards

There are a great many three card spreads, as if people consider three the perfect number for a Tarot reading—enough to look at varied aspects of the question, not so many as to get unwieldy. Here are some popular ones:

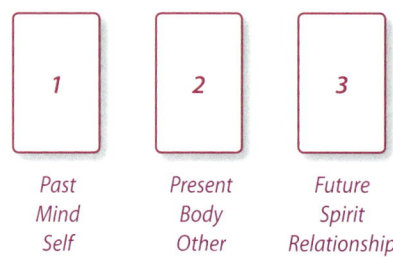

Past	Present	Future
Mind	Body	Spirit
Self	Other	Relationship

All of them can be adapted to a time of prophecy just by shifting how we look at the cards. Not just *my* Future, but the Future of the world around me. Still, it would be good to choose some spreads especially suited for the purpose of charting our way through times of cataclysm and rebirth. Again, we can work from the viewpoint of looking at the shifting moment, and what it demands of us.

Some years ago a Tarotist and my friend named Zoe Matoff came up with a spread that I have found very useful in many situations. I often use it as a daily spread. The first card goes in the middle then the second on the left and the third on the right.

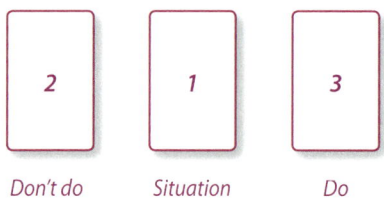

| Don't do | Situation | Do |

Simply, card 1 says something about what is going on in your life, or about whatever you have asked, card 2 an unhelpful approach, and 3 one that will be beneficial. Usually I would use this for relationship issues (I often turn to it if I'm in conflict with someone), decisions about how to spend my time, and just for the day. But let's consider it as a way to guide us through serious transformation. Then it becomes

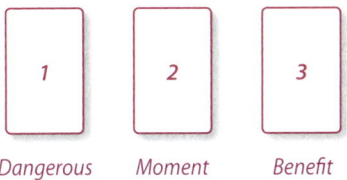

We can extend this reading by placing a new card under 1, with the idea of the new moment that can emerge from the present. We can call this "What can come" out of the situation. And then we can look at Danger and Benefit for that one, and so on.

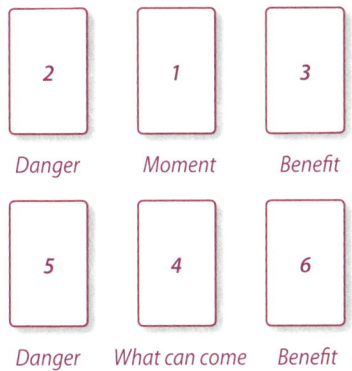

Theoretically, you can do this 26 times! That's how many lines of three there are in a seventy-eight card deck. In my opinion, however, to go beyond two or three lines runs the risk of becoming trivial, since the further we go from the present moment the more tenuous the patterns become.

A three card spread
based on a famous statement about responsibility

Two thousand years ago, at the time of Jesus, the Ancient Judae-
ans faced a true time of cataclysmic change. Rome had conquered
their nation and was trying to force them to conform to Roman
ways. An attempted revolt, in which they believed God would lead
them to victory, resulted in the destruction of the great Temple, the
very center of their religion. Huge movements were taking shape
in these shifting times. The various sects of Christianity were form-
ing that would later coalesce into a powerful religion to change the
world. Even aside from that emergence, a great spiritual vacuum
saw the rise of the rabbis, a movement based on study and devotion
and prayer rather than the ritual sacrifices performed for so long by
the inherited tribe of priests. It is hard for us, who have inherited
the Judaism that emerged from this time, to grasp what a radical
change this was. One scholar I know told me once that it took eight
hundred years for the rabbis to truly solidify their position.

One of the greatest of the early rabbis, a contemporary of Jesus,
addressed the dilemma of the individual in times of danger and
huge change. His name was Hillel, and he asked three questions
that can form the basis for a powerful reading. Hillel wrote "If I
am not for myself, who will be? If I am for myself alone, what am
I? And if not now, when?" Here is the reading I have formed from
these statements:

1. *How do I need to be for myself in this moment?*
2. *How do I need to be for others?*
3. *What must I do, right now?*

As Without, So Within

The famous expression, As Above, so Below, derived from the beginning of the Emerald Tablet sets out the daring idea that the seemingly random events and qualities of our lives actually match the

patterns of the heavens, especially as outlined in astrology. When we work with oracles and oracular devices we can lay out another principle, As Without, so Within. This means that the events and situation of the moment for any individual person are connected to the larger events and situations of the wider world. In normal times, when the outer world remains stable, this is something we do not really notice, or need to know. But in times of great change and transformation, if we want to use the Tarot as a guide through a world that is both dangerous and full of possibilities, a spread that looks at both the personal and the larger moment can be of value.

Here is a spread (its shape is up to you) that moves back and forth between "without" and "within."

1. *What is happening in the wider world?*
2. *What do I need to know about it?*
3. *What is happening in my personal world?*
4. *What do I need to know about it?*
5. *How does the outside world affect me?*
6. *What response do I need to make?*
7. *How do I affect the world?*
8. *What response do I need to make?*
9. *How will the outer world shift?*
10. *How will my personal world shift?*

Symbols of Change

Johannes Fiebig

Positive and Negative

Sometimes it will be worth it to pay your special attention to the fact that you really recognize "positive" *and* "negative" sides for each card. That doesn't mean that you have an interpretation for a card that either has a plus or a minus as premises. *The Hermit,* for instance, stands for being alone, and this you would find convenient at the one time and inconvenient at the other. This is not the point. It is rather that you realize from the very first look at the card the different aspects and meanings in this picture. *The Hermit,* for

example, is from one point of view grey all over, which means that this picture stands for a grey and dull everyday life; on the other hand, the *Hermit* is especially capable to transport light, dignity, and wisdom into everyday life. On the one hand he expresses loneliness, and on the other hand self-reliance, and so on.

Look at the image of the *Star:* one foot of the depicted figure stands on the water. In one perception, the water *carries* the foot and the whole person. In another perception, the water *denies* the access; the foot cannot get in at all, the water is kind of frozen.

Double faces …

Each image of the cards may be seen as a picture puzzle. A very special case of picture puzzle is the *Six of Cups.*

The little woman on the right has two faces. One face is looking up to the little man or dwarf (in this case, the yellow part of her head shows her hair; on the left side of this, we see her profiled face; and on the right side of her hair, there is her headscarf). The other face shows the exact opposite: she is turning away, looking down on the ground (in this case, the yellow part of her head shows her face; on the left side and on the right side of her hair, there is her headscarf). This double face refers to an important topic of the medieval iconology: The figure of *vanitas* (Latin for vanity, and emptiness)—this symbolic figure was showing a young woman at the frontside and either an old woman or a skeleton / the Death at her backside.

For the *Six of Cups,* this means: There are two looks and views of the soul. Affection and aversion, sympathy and antipathy. Both are necessary. In personal, emotional, and intimate matters, we should have both perspectives and the abilities to choose between "yes" and "no". But very often we see only one face of the depicted figure, and also in real life we are looking for just one aim, either for acceptance or for distance. If we enact both perspectives, the inner waters of the soul will have slope and tension, so they may flow well. Only in this picture the cups contain blossoms: The beauty of a vivid spirit.

... open doors in a greater reality

This double face of the Six of Cups is unique. In general, however, each card offers two or more perceptions. The hatchings in the *Three of Swords* for example may symbolize either rain or a mirror glass; etc.

If you check on your experience with each card, you will probably find out that for most of the cards these various ways of looking at them may become clear to you. There remains, however, some cards, you cannot identify as easily as others. And finally, there will be a small number of cards remaining that will lead you to the conclusion that you cannot see more than one side of that picture at all. According to all experiences it will show that with almost each Tarot-player remains a persistant rest group of cards, which are kind of a blind spot to them. It varies individually very much *which* cards these are, except the few cards (like *10 of Swords* or *The Star*) which suggest a one-sided negative or positive way of perception caused by collective habits of looking at things.

If you recognize these special cards for yourself, you recognize something very precious and helpful. They refer to the *shadow* in the psychological sense, which is explained by Ernst (see p. 43).

Practical advice: These cards, which show your blind spots of perception, you should memorize first: Neither forget them nor search too quickly for the missing explanation. According to my experience these blind spots of perception exist in everybody, of course even without the Tarot-cards. That means the Tarot-pictures do not produce the one-sided perception of a certain situation, but they demonstrate them. Usually remarkable subjects of personal self-experience hide or slumber behind them. It will be most effective to memorize these pictures, like you do it with certain key-dreams, to live with them for a while, until you notice why you had this lack of perception and what this means to you.

Take your time. In the end, these personal subjects that were living in the inner shadow formerly, will guide you in a new, good, greater future. For they show old lumber, that now you know may define and delete. Or unused talents, which will guide you to a new fortune as now you know about their existence. As Arthur E. Waite said in his *Pictorial Key to the Tarot (p. 89).* "The pictures are like doors which open into unexpected chambers, or like a turn in the open road with a wide prospect beyond."

Tarot
for Magical Times

78 Cards
Messages and Advices

12 Months / 36 Decans
The Qualities of Time

The Fool

Some see him as the beginning of the Major Arcana and some see him as the end. In reality, it depends on how the *Fool—you*—move through crises and challenging times of the world or your own life. Originally this card meant a crazy homeless person, driven from place to place, often attacked by animals. If you have lost everything, if your world has collapsed around you, then the *Fool* can mirror this difficult state—alone, with nothing left but what you can carry in a bag on a stick.

But look at the picture. Does he appear miserable? The other meaning of the *Fool* is freedom—freedom from rules, freedom from possessions, freedom from all narrow beliefs of what is important, even your own previous beliefs about yourself. His number, 0, means no-thing, no limitations. The *Fool* has learned to react to everything exactly as it is, not as what he thinks it *should* be. By accepting drastic change, he gains freedom.

Divinatory meanings: Spontaneity, freedom, taking risks. Difficulty in planning ahead.
Reversed: Hesitation, fear of risk. Possibly caution, preparation.
Action: A moment to act spontaneously, without plans or even thought.

The Magician

Originally a very tricky fellow, a kind of sly carnival figure who plays a game with the suit objects on his table, the *Magician* has become a grand "magus" who brings the heavenly power of Above down into the physical world. The infinity sign above his head reminds us that he is the first figure to manifest—make real—the *Fool's* infinite possibilities. He treats life and its crises as a creative art.

On his table lie the objects of the Minor Arcana, the Wand (the stick, not the crystal wand he holds up), the Cup, the Sword, and the Pentacle. Because he is focused and clear he can draw on all the elements, be master of every situation. To borrow from the I Ching, he is the primary *yang* card, the principle of action.

Divinatory meanings: Clear and focused, tricky. Able to handle any situation. Getting this card means you can act magically in a crisis and in times of changes, doing things that might seem impossible.
Reversed: Confusion. Difficulty focusing your energy. It might be necessary to wait rather than act in the moment.
Action: Focused will can transform a situation.

The High Priestess

She sits mysteriously between a dark and light pillar, as if poised between powerful forces that might otherwise threaten to tear her apart. She is *yin* to the *Magician's yang*, the principle of perfect stillness. She suggests that right now the best thing to do is stay calm, be at peace, and do nothing while everything (or every*one*) rages around you. You can practice this in daily life. At work, or in a restaurant, or with your family, take a few seconds to sit or stand perfectly still, eyes closed if possible, and be aware that everything swirls around you without actually touching you.The scroll in her lap remains rolled up for she does not teach, or explain, or lead. She represents those moments when we know something with perfect clarity but can't explain it or even put it into words.

Divinatory meanings: Silence, stillness, the ability—and necessity—to stay calm in extreme situations. Inner peace, spiritual mystery.

Reversed: Moving towards passion, emotional involvement. Sharing knowledge or feelings with the people around you. A need to act on something.

Action: Stay silent. Not a time for action or communication.

The Empress

One of the Tarot's happiest, most passionate cards, she represents lushness and fertility (some see her as pregnant, but I will leave that to your judgment). The woman symbol on her heart shaped shield is, in fact, the astrological sign for the planet Venus, named for the Roman goddess of love (the male sign actually signifies Mars). She urges us to embrace life in hard times, to trust that love will transcend suffering. Her tiara contains twelve stars, for the zodiac, making her a *Regina Coeli*, a Queen of Heaven, while the trees, and the flowing river, and especially the golden grain growing all around her simple loveseat "throne," show her attachment to nature. Pomegranates decorate her face. Filled with seeds, and juice the color of blood, pomegranates not only symbolize fertility, they actually contain estrogen, the female hormone, as well as chemicals that help prevent cancer.

Divinatory meanings: Passion, fertility, optimism. A reminder to embrace life in harsh moments. She can represent love, but also motherhood.

Reversed: Caution. The need to think and plan rather than act from emotion.

Action: A moment to express your passion with great confidence.

The Emperor

Many people do not like this card. They find him harsh, aggressive, controlling. The lush forest of the *Empress* has changed to barren mountains, her soft couch to a gray throne, and the river that gushed behind her now becomes a thin stream barely able to cut its way through the rocks. He seems uncaring, emotionless, dressed in a suit of armor underneath his imperial robes. He represents government, society, and sometime a harsh father.

And yet, so much of this looks at him from *outside*, a figure that looms over us and demands obedience. But if we can see ourselves as the *Emperor*—and women can do this as well as men—then he teaches us to defend our territory and our families, to set up structures so that life can continue. Sometimes the *Emperor* is exactly what we need to be.

Divinatory meanings: Power, authority, control. Social structures, government officials. The ability to defend something, or to take a position of authority. Can mean fatherhood.
Reversed: His rigidity softens, he becomes more compassionate, but possibly weak. Difficulty exerting authority.
Action: Take charge. Defend what is valuable to you.

The Hierophant

The picture shows a pope (the card's original title) but the name describes the person who directed the ancient mystery rituals of death and rebirth. Thus the card suggests both the outer level of tradition—something to believe in during hard times—but also the possibility of esoteric, or secret teachings. Though the image is clearly Christian it can refer to any traditional teaching, even family traditions, that can help give us direction. On the other hand, the *Hierophant* tends to expect, even demand, obedience and conformity, as if we are all his disciples. He leaves little room for people to develop their own ideas, or make their own decisions. The *Emperor* and the *Hierophant* together represent the power of authority, the *Emperor* through laws and the *Hierophant* through teaching. Because priests perform weddings the *Hierophant* sometimes signifies marriage.

Divinatory meanings: Tradition, especially religious teachings that give comfort or direction. Conformity to traditional ways of acting and teaching. Obedience to authority. Possibly marriage.
Reversed: Going your own way. Rebellion against tradition. Shallowness or gullibility.
Action: Find a lesson in traditional teachings. A time to conform.

The Lovers

Older versions of this card showed a young man between two women, as if he must choose between them. As a result, many people see "Choice" as the primary theme for trump Six, and if we look at Tarot in times of great change then this card may warn us of important decisions, with the need to choose wisely. Only—those old pictures show Cupid about to shoot an arrow at the young man, implying not only that the choice may involve relationships, but also that he will choose by emotion rather than careful consideration.

The current version shows an angel blessing a man and a woman. Thus it becomes a fulfilling relationship rather than choice. Or does it? The couple are, in fact, Adam and Eve, but blessed rather than condemned, as if they have made the *right* choices. Notice that Adam looks to Eve and Eve looks to the angel. Masculine consciousness (*yang*) must travel through feminine inner wisdom (*yin*) to reach the highest levels.

Divinatory meanings: **A strong relationship, especially romantic. Or an important choice.**
Reversed: **A time to act alone. Be careful of bad choices.**
Action: **Experience the spiritual power of love and relationship.**

The Chariot

After the image of a strong relationship in the *Lovers,* we find three cards that show how individuals might handle great change, either in their own lives or the world around them. The *Chariot* indicates the way of a strong will. Now is a moment to take charge of a situation with great confidence, to see crisis as opportunity. The sphinxes look in opposite directions, symbolic of contradictions that might pull apart a situation. The Charioteer holds them together through force of personality.

Subtle symbols of the previous cards permeate the image, such as the magic wand he holds, or the star crown that recalls the *Empress.* He has learned how to make use of different qualities to succeed. In ancient times kings and generals rode through the streets in chariots to receive the acclaim of the people. Thus, the card indicates victory, recognition.

Divinatory meanings: **Strong will that overcomes problems rather than solves them. Success. Possibly isolation.**
Reversed: **Doubt, weakness. Sometimes, asking for help or seeing support.**
Action: **A time to act without doubt or hesitation.**

Strength

This gentle card shows an alternative to the *Chariot's* willpower. Early decks showed Hercules killing a lion, symbolic of virtue overcoming lust. Here the woman does not hurt the lion but gently tames him. He licks her hand like a puppy, his tail between his legs. The infinity sign above her head links her to the *Magician's* ability to draw down divine energy, but also tells us that genuine strength is never-ending. When you get this card, ask what strength means to you (or ask the questioner if you are reading for someone else). Some people see it as the ability to do the right thing, others as taming their inner demons.

Because she does not kill or cage the lion some see the card as a symbol of the environmental movement. In natural disasters or other emergencies those who protect animals often seem to carry a great strength.

Divinatory meanings: Inner strength, gentleness, great confidence without the need to prove yourself. Connection with animals.

Reversed: Doubt, weakness, feeling cut off from whatever nourishes you. Sometimes, asking for help.

Action: Use gentle strength to tame a dangerous situation.

The Hermit

To everything there is a season. The Tarot teaches us that there is a time to charge ahead and a time to hold back. A time to be with others and a time to be alone. If we hope to move forward and conquer, like the *Chariot* or the *Knight of Swords,* then we may not welcome this lonely figure on his mountaintop. The *Fool* steps joyously off his cliff, unconcerned with what will happen. The Hermit makes no move, only holds up his light. And if we hope for love, and a deep relationship then here too the Hermit will disappoint us. But the lonely *Hermit* may be just what we need. Until the times change, and the Tarot tells us to act, or get involved with others, what might we learn by going into ourselves?

Sometimes the *Hermit* signals someone other than the questioner. He may represent a guide, or a wise teacher, not necessarily a man, and not necessarily old.

Divinatory meanings: Being alone. Maturity and wisdom. A teacher or spiritual guide.

Reversed: Becoming more active, more involved with other people. Possibly immaturity.

Action: A time to withdraw from involvement, but be willing to lead when others are ready.

The Wheel of Fortune

If we see the Tarot as a prophecy of great change, and spiritually as a Book of Changes to guide us through such intense times, then the *Wheel of Fortune* plays a vital role. Halfway through the Major Arcana the Wheel gives us a vision of everything in flux, of fate turning the wheel, whether we want it to or not. As if to remind us how mysterious life can be, the card abounds with symbolic images— mythological creatures, Hebrew and European letters, alchemical signs. They all have precise meanings. For example, the four winged figures derive from medieval images of the four "evangelists," Mathew, Mark, Luke, and John (thus the books that they hold). They also represent the four "fixed" signs of the zodiac, and thus the constantly changing seasons. We could decode every detail but the effect would remain, a vision of life's mysteries and a reminder that we do not control what happens.

Divinatory meanings: Fate, the turning wheel of life. Something is about to change. Taking a chance.
Reversed: Delays when we expect something to change. Confusion. Trying to resist fate.
Action: Accept the turns of fate. Do not try to control events.

Justice

If the *Wheel of Fortune* represents what we cannot control, then *Justice* challenges us to look closely at who we are, what we have done. Unlike most courthouse statues of *Justice* she does not wear a blindfold (compare the *Two of Swords*), but stares directly at us, a challenge to say the truth. The sword points straight up, one of only three to do so, along with the *Ace* and *Queen of Swords*. It reminds us that Justice requires action, not just passive observation. We need to understand, and then do what is right.

As card eleven, *Justice* is pivotal, the beginning of the second half of the Major Arcana (0-10, 11-21). In times of changes and challenges it tells us two things. First, we cannot avoid the truth, we need to look at our own part in everything. Second, we need to make a decision and act upon it, with principle and fairness as our guides.

Divinatory meanings: Truth, honesty, self-acceptance. Fairness. The need to act justly. A just outcome in a court case.
Reversed: Lack of balance, blaming others for our own choices. Possible bias in a legal issue.
Action: A time for complete honesty. You must act as an agent of Justice.

X-The Wheel of Fortune • XI-Justice

The Hanged Man

Here we find one of the Tarot's most mysterious cards, with interpretations that range from execution to spiritual enlightenment! In Italy people sometimes hanged traitors upside down, and thus some decks call him "L'Appeso," the Traitor. Coming between *Justice* and *Death*, he could indeed represent a hanged *criminal*, though a traitor to some may be a hero to others. Less dramatically, some see him as stuck, unable to move without some painful sacrifice. Yet radiant light fills his face, an image we find nowhere else in the deck. The positive side shows an attachment to our deepest values, a spiritual connection as strong as an ancient tree. We may appear wrong to others, upside down, but we have found our own truth. Whatever crisis or great change surrounds us, we can remain calm and radiant.

Divinatory meanings: As the reader, you get to decide how you see this card—stuck in a bad situation, or attachment to deep values? Maybe we should look for the light that shines in the questioner's face.

Reversed: Allowing others' opinions to sway your actions. Or getting unstuck.

Action: Action is not possible right now. Resist pressure from others by attachment to your deepest values.

Death

Just by the name, this is one of the deck's more fearsome cards. If we look at the Tarot as a book of prophecy, or a guide in times of upheaval, it's tempting to see card Thirteen—unnamed in earlier decks—as a prediction of physical death, either personally or on a large scale. In modern Tarot, however, we see this card more as dramatic change. *Something* dies, but not necessarily the body. A pattern, a way of life, a bad marriage, or a dead end job.

The figures around *Death* symbolize the ways we face such shifts. Look at the white haired king and the child. The dead king represents the ego that clings to what it knows and cannot let go. The child, on the other hand, shows openness to whatever will happen. He welcomes the rider on the black horse with flowers.

Divinatory meanings: Usually not a card of physical death, but rather of dramatic change. The end of something. Acceptance leads to new life.

Reversed: Resisting change, clinging to old ways. Something we thought over shows new life.

Action: A moment to release whatever you cling to. Be like a child as things change around you.

Temperance

Coming after the release of *Death, Temperance* shows a powerful angel, as if we have found the truest part of ourselves. One of the medieval "cardinal virtues" (along with *Justice* and *Strength*), *Temperance* means to take a middle way, to stay calm in the midst of fear and danger. When we get this card we need to realize that the Tarot is not simply saying "This would be a good idea, you should do this." Instead, it tells us that we *can* stay centered and focused, despite danger or upheavals all around us. And in fact we can use the card as a tool to do just that. If you find yourself spinning out of control, giving way to fear or anger, picture the card of *Temperance* (you might even carry it around with you). Imagine yourself as the angel, confident and strong, pouring water magically from one cup to another.

*Divinatory meanings: **Calm and confidence in the midst of crisis. A middle way between extremes. Sobriety.***

*Reversed: **Swings of emotion or behavior. Losing your sense of self. Drunkenness.***

*Action: **A moment when you can find magical power in calmness and concentration.***

The Devil

With the *Devil* the Tarot's prophetic sequence comes into full force. He symbolizes the light that now is imprisoned and needs release. In individual readings as well, we can see him as whatever seems to trap people in fear or obsession. The *Devil's* number, 15, "reduces" to 6 (1+5=6). Put the two cards side by side and you will see how the Devil appears to corrupt the *Lovers'* perfect harmony. Instead of an angel blessing Adam and Eve, we see a scowling monster who keeps his slaves chained to his block of stone. But look closely. The loops of the chains are large enough for them to take them off and walk away. In reality, the card teaches the opposite of what it seems. The moment we stop believing in our helplessness is the moment of our freedom. Some people take a very different view and see the *Devil* as simply a wild time, letting loose after Temperance's perfect control.

*Divinatory meanings: **Darkness, fear, situations or addictions that seem to enslave us. Alternatively, wild time, excess.***

*Reversed: **Seeing through illusions. Liberation. Recovery from addiction—or, the day after a wild party.***

*Action: **A time to go into darkness and discover what is hidden there.***

The Tower

On the Tarot's prophetic level of great and sudden change this is the climactic moment. What will happen happens here. The picture appears disastrous, even terrifying, as lightning strikes a grim stone tower and people seemingly are thrown from the high windows to what looks like destruction below. And yet, if we look at the symbols the ultimate message, as with the *Devil,* becomes one of liberation. The drops of light, or fire, take the form of the Hebrew letter *yod*, the beginning of God's most powerful name (see around the rim of the *Wheel of Fortune*). Appearing also on the Aces of Wands, Cups, and Swords, the *yods*—twenty-two of them, for the number of cards in the Major Arcana—represent divine grace. Not just in the larger world, but in our individual lives we sometimes find ourselves oppressed, seemingly trapped. At such times we may need something to shake us loose, to free us, even if it feels like lightning has struck and everything has fallen apart.

Divinatory meanings: Upheaval, sudden change, a shock. Also, revelation, discovery.
Reversed: Similar, but not as extreme. Possibly a refusal to accept a shocking discovery.
Action: Do not try to resist drastic change, allow it to free you.

The Star

After the stormy *Tower* comes one of the Tarot's loveliest cards. This is the calm after great change, the discovery of new hope, whether it comes after a drastic planetary shift, or a personal upheaval, for example. There are still difficult times ahead—the wilderness journey of the *Moon*—but the Star tells us to trust. Unlike Temperance, where an angel carefully pours water from one cup to another, the Star maiden holds nothing back. The *Star's* number, 17, reduces to 8, *Strength*, a link hinted at by all the stars having eight points. In her, we find our inner strength and belief.

In the Tarot as a Book of Changes—a guide to the challenges and lessons of the moment—the *Star* teaches us to accept whatever is, to drop all our shields, to believe. On another level the water poured out can signify healing, emotional but also physical.

Divinatory meanings: Hope, openness, especially after a crisis. Renewal, healing, restoration.
Reversed: Holding back, difficulty opening up emotionally. Possibly a need to hide your true feelings.
Action: A time of great hope and renewal. Don't be afraid to shine for others.

The Moon

The *Moon* represents the wilderness, the uncertain journey between the calm openness of the *Star* and the bright clarity of the
Sun. Under the *Moon's* reflected light psychic abilities awaken,
but also fear and strange feelings. For the first time we see no
people in the card, only animals, a dog and a wolf howling or
yelping at the strange light, and a crayfish half emerging from agitated water.
Here in unknown territory our animal selves take over. We cannot suppress the
wild emotions but only travel through them.

In the Tarot as prophecy the *Moon* signifies the dangerous time between the
end of one world structure and the beginning of another. On the emotional
level it can indicate the strange state when something powerful has ended and
you find yourself thrown back on your instincts. The *Moon* card calls forth other
qualities as well—powerful dreams, visions, and the power of the feminine.

*Divinatory meanings: **Wildness, uncharted territory. Strong dreams, psychic abilities***
*Reversed: **Coming to the end of a difficult time. The need to accept your wild animal self.***
*Action: **Listen to your dreams, your animal instincts. Do not try to analyze what is hap-
pening.***

The Sun

Under the *Moon,* the world appears strange and mysterious. The
Sun brings clarity, simplicity. The animal self has now joined with
the human, a mild horse carrying a joyous child waving a red
banner. Traditionally, the *Sun* signifies rationality compared to
the irrational untamed wilderness of the *Moon*. For the Tarot as
prophecy—and in personal matters as well—this is the moment when a new
world, a new life, begins to take shape. The path becomes clear as we see what
we need to do. The number 19 reduces to 10 (1+9), the *Wheel of Fortune,* for the
great shifts in the world, but then reduces once more to 1 (1+0), the *Magician,*
sign of a new beginning. If we see the Tarot as a Book of Changes the *Sun* tells
us to act boldly, with clarity of purpose, but also trust. Not the confidence of a
warrior, but the openness of a child.

*Divinatory meanings: **Happiness, clarity, simplicity, moving forward towards a new life.
Good health.***
*Reversed: **The card retains its positive nature, but with some doubt or confusion, as if
clouds temporarily cover the Sun.***
*Action: **Bring mysteries into the light.***

Judgment

The title and the image of this card derive from the Christian idea of the Last Judgment, when the angel summons the dead from their graves, some to ascend to Heaven but most to fall into the pits of hell. As a result, many people find the card frightening. But if you look carefully you will see that no one is being judged. They all open their arms joyously to the trumpet as it brings them from "death" to a new beginning.

In the prophecy for magical times this is the moment of true change, a new and more spiritual consciousness emerging from the wreck of the old world. This is the most *populated* card, seven figures if we include the angel. The changes it shows affect everyone. When any one of us becomes transformed the world around us—families, friends, even society—cannot help but change as well.

Divinatory meanings: Great change, renewal. A sense that we are called to rise up and live our lives in a different way. Family or a relationship restored.

Reversed: Resistance to change. Difficulty in believing in something that has started.

Action: Pay attention to signs and inner hints of a transformation.

The World

The climactic card of the Major Arcana also becomes the climax of the Tarot as prophecy. Here we see the *World* restored, or a new world fully emerged. The elegant dancer appears in the blue sky, as if our consciousness no longer needs the ground of our old beliefs and prejudices, what we considered reality. She dances in a wreath of victory, oval-shaped, like an egg out of which something truly new and wonderful will burst forth. The oval form also reminds us of the *Fool,* with his number zero to symbolize infinite possibilities. Here we see the realization of everything hinted at in the *Fool,* and yet, almost miraculously, the *World* does not limit us but rather shows us a life even more filled with potential.

The figures in the corner may remind us of the *Wheel of Fortune.* There we saw strange cartoon-like forms along with mysterious symbols. Here everything has become realistic, understood in its full beauty.

Divinatory meanings: Success, satisfaction, a spiritual and practical sense of achievement. Wondrous new possibilities.

Reversed: Setbacks and delays rather than failure. Stable structures, security.

Action: This is a moment when all things are possible.

XX-Judgment • XXI-The World

Ace of Wands

A white hand emerges out of a gray cloud, as if purpose and firm action come forward out of confusion. The hand holds the emblem of the suit, a stick with leaves, the one emblem that's not man-made. This gives the suit a simplicity, uncomplicated by emotions or ideas (Cups and Swords) or monetary and practical considerations (Pentacles). This is the suit of Fire, basic life energy, with the *Ace* as its purest form. This card reminds us we're alive, even in great crisis. It tells us that even as the world might burn, life goes on, and we can do something, have an effect. Don't analyze or worry, don't agonize or calculate, just take the first step.

The falling leaves take the form of the Hebrew letter *yod* (see *Tower* and *Aces of Cups* and *Swords*), symbol that life comes to us as a continuing gift.

Divinatory meanings: **Life energy, potency, sexual vitality. Action in a crisis. The promise of restoration.**

Reversed: **Weakness, doubt, hesitation. Sometimes delays or setbacks.**

Action: **A moment of energy and vitality. Seize the initiative.**

Two of Wands

A well-dressed man stands on what looks like a castle wall. He holds one Wand as if ready to use it, maybe as a walking stick if he will leave his castle in search of adventure. The other, however, stands bolted to the wall, symbol of responsibilities, security, safety, whatever might hold him back. He holds a globe in his hands. Does it represent his desire for action, or his fears of global disaster? The *Ace* kept everything simple, pure energy, action. *Two* brings in choice, and thus doubt. In a crisis, with everything shifting or gone, do you try to protect what you have, or do you go forth into a new world that might be emerging from the breakdown of the old? In more everyday situations the card can show the dilemma of someone who has used Wands' fire energy to build a life, but now that energy seeks new things.

Divinatory meanings: **Choosing between security and adventure, responsibility or desire.**

Reversed: **Danger of opportunity passing. The choice becomes more immediate. Regret.**

Action: **A time to decide between security and new possibilities. Both decisions are valid.**

Three of Wands

We can look at each suit as a continuing story. With Wands the tale concerns someone energetic and strong, who tries to solve the problems all around him with individual action but has trouble joining with others, and with the responsibilities his actions end up creating. In the *Two* we saw someone making a choice. Here he has left security behind and ventures into the dangerous world.

People often ask about the difference between the *Two* and *Three*. Both show a man holding a Wand and looking out over water. In the Two, however, he remains in the castle. This man stands on a hilltop, alone, like the *Hermit*. Notice his patchwork clothing. Has he lost his wealth in the cataclysm, or simply put everything into a daring venture? Do you see the boats in the water? They can symbolize the risks he takes. Or maybe he has sent his family to safety while he remains behind, alone, to face disasters and opportunities.

Divinatory meanings: **New ventures, risk, acting alone. Sending something into the world.**
Reversed: **Working with others, cooperation.**
Action: **Commitment to new things, a new path.**

Four of Wands

In the movement of the *Wands* suit the middle cards, *Four, Five,* and *Six,* show a dramatic change from the rest. While *One-Three* and *Seven-Ten* show a single figure, the middle three bring in community. They also are probably the most positive, as if Wands energy, so individualistic and heroic in a crisis, actually finds its greatest fulfillment when it overcomes its tendency to act alone and impulsively, or to take on solitary burdens.

While *Five* and *Six* contain their own virtues, *Four* is the happiest scene in the suit. In the other suits the *Three* tends to show a kind of early optimism, but here it's the *Four*. We see a celebration, two figures in the front holding up flowers, while behind them people dance or move in procession. Because the bower resembles a wedding canopy found in some traditions, many see this card as a hint of marriage. In fact, it matters less what they celebrate than the fact they do it as a group.

Divinatory meanings: **Celebration, community, joy. Break from struggle.**
Reversed: **Traditionally, the meanings remain the same.**
Action: **Celebrate, especially with family and community.**

Five of Wands

From the joyous *Four* the energy shifts once again, to competition. Compare this image to the solitary *Three*. Fire contains a strong individualist streak. It wants to strive, to take on new things. Even the end of the old world becomes an exciting opportunity. All the *Fives* show struggle or hardship, but the Wands turns that harsh energy into an exciting battle to do new things. Five young men either fight with sticks or try to build something. If a fight, no one really wants to hurt anyone, just to let loose some pent-up energy, like boys play-fighting. But if they are trying to actually accomplish something, especially build something new in the midst of breakdown, then the lack of a leader can mean chaos. In the idea of Tarot as prophecy this card can indicate the first steps to rebuild the world—optimistic, full of life, yet clumsy and without direction.

Divinatory meanings: Struggle, competition, even fighting, but all of it with a positive attitude. An energetic atmosphere at work, or with a group of people.

Reversed: The competition becomes harsher, more aggressive. People may act behind someone's back.

Action: A time to enjoy competition, even if group activity becomes chaotic.

Six of Wands

As described in the *Four,* the middle three cards of the suit show communal scenes. Imagine a breakdown of society and then the emergence of a new energy. The *Four* showed people finding community and hope, the *Five* gave us excited, but chaotic attempts to build something. In the *Six* a leader emerges, the classic Man On A Horse who inspires others to gather around him. He wears a wreath of victory on his head and carries another on his Wand. His horse is decorated as if for a parade, while the others walk alongside.

While this card appears overwhelmingly positive, both for the confident leader and his followers, the idea of Tarot as a Book of Changes warns us that such moments carry danger. On a large scale the desire for a Great Leader can lead to fascism, while on the more individual level it separates the strong person from those around him.

Divinatory meanings: Optimism, triumph, the ability to inspire others, especially their trust and loyalty.

Reversed: Negativity, doubt. Possibly acting alone, or keeping your plans a secret.

Action: Let yourself lead and inspire others.

Seven of Wands

The energy of Wands shifts back to individual action, as if the Way of Fire has tried a communal approach but really wants to operate alone, or even as one against the world. We see a young man on a hilltop, wearing mismatched shoes, as if he got dressed in a hurry to go out and battle—what? What lurks below remains hidden, though most see it as an implied group of attackers, and the man as a courageous defender. Some of the Wands figures may remind us of the Survivalist approach to planetary crisis: Expect society to collapse (for one reason or another) and prepare by creating a sanctuary far from cities, where they will bring their families and fight off anyone who encroaches on their territory. Extreme? Yes, but there is something in that battling attitude that comes out in the *Seven of Wands*.

Divinatory meanings: Courage, heroism, isolation. A sense of one against the world.

Reversed: Possibly weakness or defeat, but also could be seeking a more cooperative approach.

Action: This is a time to separate from others, to rise above the group.

Eight of Wands

The *Eight of Wands* is possibly the most mysterious card in the Rider Tarot. This is because it is the only card where no people or animals appear. The *Aces* show a hand, and the *Three of Swords* the icon of a heart, but here the *eight Wands* fly through the air all by themselves. Judging by the placement of the leaves they point downwards, as if launched by some heavenly force and now about to come to Earth. They move in parallel, suggesting an alignment of energies. But whose energies? Who has launched them, and for what purpose? Maybe they hint at a return to group effort, problems solved when people are able to work in harmony. And maybe the lack of figures, indicates people who act anonymously, seeking only the common good.

Or maybe its strangeness hints at something more radical—the idea of invisible forces coming to our aid. We see their effects but not the forces themselves.

Divinatory meanings: Action, movement. People joining together for a common good. Higher forces acting in the world.

Reversed: A situation continues without a clear end. People have trouble working together.

Action: Be aware of varied things coming together, of people uniting.

Nine of Wands

The Wands suit carries a tension between group activity and individual action. Here we see someone who battles life's problems all alone, able to stand his ground no matter what. And yet, he pays a price. He grips his stick tightly, either for support or as a weapon to ward off any new attacks. We might imagine him as the survivalist from *Seven*, a few years later, when his battles have taken a toll. His right shoulder hunches up in tension while his arm blocks his chest. The bandage around his head suggests a psychic wound. He looks over his shoulder at—what? Do the other Wands represent enemies or threats? Or has he fought so long that he now searches for enemies only he can see? Another, more positive reading, would notice the gap in the row of Wands, as if the one he holds comes from there, and suggest the nine symbolize his resources.

Divinatory meanings: Strength, heroic action. An emotional or physical price someone might pay for a long struggle.
Reversed: Weakness, possibly defeat, but also a suggestion to let go of defensiveness.
Action: A moment to stand firm rather than walk away or seek solutions.

Ten of Wands

In this card we see both the strength and the limitations of the Wands' approach to great change. The attempts to find community have gone, as have the resistance of *Seven* and *Nine*. What we see is someone bowed down by burdens as he attempts to carry the maximum number of sticks. There is something honorable here, even heroic, as he does what needs to be done. His way of carrying the sticks appears awkward—he would do better to tie them in a bundle and hoist them on his shoulder. But then he might crush the young leaves.

In the story of a great upheaval he represents the person who may not understand what has happened, or the spiritual consciousness that emerges, but simply dedicates himself to whatever needs to be done so that others may flourish. At the same time, service to others can result in exploitation or loneliness.

Divinatory meanings: Burdens, dedication, hard work. Possibly sacrifice of self for others' well-being.
Reversed: Release from burdens. Getting help or asking that others take a greater role.
Action: Accept burdens for the sake of others.

Page of Wands

A jaunty, rather feminine *Page* stands in a desert—are they pyramids or simply sand dunes?—where he tilts back his head as he holds his Wand firmly if a bit awkwardly. In general, the *Pages* approach the great challenges of crisis and change with eagerness and excitement. This becomes especially true for Fiery Wands, and this card encourages us to see life's challenges, even danger, as opportunity. Experience, knowledge, even skill, are not necessary, only openness and desire.

Traditional divination describes *Pages* as messengers. The message of Fire tells us to take on life's problems without worry about the likelihood of success. Another divinatory tradition sees this *Page's* message as about love—perhaps an email or Facebook message? The circular lizards on the Page's tunic are salamanders, the elemental animal of Fire, found also on the Knight and King. With most the tails do not touch the mouths, symbolizing incompletion.

Divinatory meanings: **Eagerness, excitement, a young attitude to challenges. Messages, possibly of love.**
Reversed: **Hesitation, worry, conscious of challenges. Possibly an unfaithful lover.**
Action: **Be ready to begin something, to declare your willingness.**

Knight of Wands

As described in the introduction, we can look at Court cards as themselves a Book of Changes—not so much a tool to identify other people, but rather a shifting kaleidoscope of ways we face great challenges. Here we see the power of adventure and animal energy. People sometimes look at this card and assume the horse is charging ahead. In fact, like the Pentacles horse, it doesn't go anywhere, but unlike that stolid horse this one rears up, as if unable to contain its power. The *Knight's* plume, and the ends of fabric on his tunic, take the form of flames.

This is the way of adventure, a desire to take on life. Where others may see a crisis or disaster he might see a chance for action. He does not temper his Knightly energy with *Cups'* empathy, or Swords' heroic dedication, or *Pentacles'* responsibility. For the *Knight of Wands* the adventure is all that matters.

Divinatory meanings: **Excitement, energy, confidence that sees danger as opportunity.**
Reversed: **Setbacks, delays, as if the untried Knight has fallen off his horse.**
Action: **Seek adventure, movement, new experience.**

Queen of Wands

We can look at so many of the Wands cards as ways in which people might respond to a world in extreme transition. Some see opportunities for adventure, some take on great responsibility, some battle to protect what they have, or their families.

The *Queen* loves life, and especially nature. She withdraws from struggle or change so that she can hold onto her optimistic view of the world. Notice the black cat before her throne, as if on guard to protect her. For some this marks her as a witch, but we also might see it as the natural world responding to her love. She holds a sunflower, as if plucked from the *Sun* card's garden. Many see her as the most sexual of the *Queens,* for she sits with her legs apart. While she may enjoy sex she doesn't seem eager for a relationship. It would only complicate her simple life.

Divinatory meanings: Love of life, simplicity. Sexual energy but not in search of relationship.

Reversed: Life challenges her, pushes her to get involved with others. She can be good in a crisis but not an extended difficulty.

Action: A time to love life, and keep everything simple.

King of Wands

Kings signify responsibility, authority, and as we have seen with several Wands cards, the Fire element likes adventure, even struggle. This *King* looks uncomfortable on his throne, leaning forward as if he would like to get up and ride off like the *Knight*. Dressed largely in red, with a gold crown shaped like flames, he loves his element—except for being bound to his throne.

And yet, despite the contradictions, he also appears as a true leader, confident and charismatic. This might be called the Wands paradox—they don't really want leadership roles, they're just good at it. The many salamanders that adorn the outside of his cloak have their tales in their mouth (compare the *Page* and the *Knight*). This symbolizes completion, the closed circle of accomplishment. While others may admire this he himself might want the circles to open up.

Divinatory meanings: Confidence, leadership, the admiration of others. Accepting responsibility or a position of authority, while secretly yearning for freedom.

Reversed: Movement away from responsibility. Harshness, possibly resentment at other people's expectations.

Action: Accept responsibility even if you would rather be on your own.

Ace of Cups

The famous white hand emerges from the gray cloud and holds forth the Cup in an open palm, the image of an outright gift. The hand comes from the right, the side of reason, and holds the Cup to the left, emotion. We respond best to this gift if we do so with feeling rather than analysis.

This is possibly the most propitious card in the Minor Arcana, and the most overtly spiritual, for the Cup is the Holy Grail, focus of Medieval Christian legends, though possibly with Pagan roots. The Grail, like the Celtic Cauldron, could heal not just the sick but the land itself, the "Wasteland," to use a famous Grail legend term. This sets up the entire theme of the suit, how we can create a new world, more spiritually alive, after the breakdown of the old. The primary message here is that the gift of spiritual and even physical healing comes to us at every moment.

Divinatory meanings: Healing, spiritual and physical. A fresh start emotionally.
Reversed: Pessimism or doubt leading to a rejection of some emotional gift.
Action: Allow emotions to overflow and bring healing.

Two of Cups

A man and woman, both of them solemn and strong, hold up their Cups to each other, with the man reaching out his hand to the woman. Between the Cups, as if generated by their joint energy, rises the ancient magical symbol of the caduceus, two snakes wound around a column. Usually wings will appear at the top, but here we see a lion's head as well, an alchemical image of transformation. Today we associate the caduceus with the medical profession, but in ancient times it belonged to Hermes, god of magic and wisdom (and according to a modern myth, creator of the Tarot itself). Modern Tarot sees this card as a romantic relationship, possibly a commitment. Here we can see something deeper, people coming together to create a new world. Notice the basic equality of the man and woman, and the energy generated between them. This new society will be one of equality and cooperation.

Divinatory meanings: People coming together in a powerful way. Dedication to a high purpose. Traditionally a romantic relationship.
Reversed: Acting alone, closing off cooperation. Disappointment in a relationship.
Action: A time to form a deep connection with someone, possibly, but not necessarily, romantic.

Three of Cups

This is a card of celebration, of community. Three women come together and raise high their Cups, as if to elevate their joy above all else. They actually resemble somewhat the caduceus of the previous card, the two snakes wound around a central column. We also might think of the three Graces, or the three Fates, or the Triple Goddess, whose worship modern Pagans have revived. We can see that this card opens up to deeper levels than just a good time. The potential of the *Two*—the possibility of a new world hinted at in the magical caduceus—seems to have come into being.

Or has it? The first three cards of the suit make it all look so easy. If we look ahead, at the *Four* and especially the *Five*, we will realize that creating a new world is not that simple. And yet, right now is the time for celebration.

Divinatory meanings: **Celebration, joy. People coming together. Women's energy and support.**

Reversed: **Separation. End of celebration, a need to look at hard realities.**

Action: **A moment to party and celebrate with friends.**

Four of Cups

A young man sits looking at three Cups in a row, arms crossed as if he rejects them somehow, while a hand emerges from a cloud to offer a fourth. The image may remind us of the *Ace*. There the hand went from right to left, an offer of healing to the emotions. Here it moves to the right, as if it tries to bring the rational self into the happiness of the previous card, the joyous *Three*. Either he just doesn't see the fourth Cup or he distrusts it. Maybe he understands that something is missing, emotion is not enough. Notice that we do not see a group of four Cups but rather three plus one. The same thing happens in the *Five*, three plus two.

Some criticize the man in the picture. They see him as negative for not taking the new Cup, or even lazy. But maybe he knows that emotion alone cannot sustain a community.

Divinatory meanings: **A question of whether to take hold of an opportunity. Someone might not see something in front of him—or he may recognize its limitations.**

Reversed: **Action overcomes passivity. Seizing an opportunity.**

Action: **Consider options carefully. Something good may be offered, but do not rush to take it.**

Five of Cups

For many this represents the low point of the suit. A figure cloaked in black stares at three spilled Cups. Two upright Cups stand behind it, and they may signify either what remains, or new possibilities. Either way, the figure seems to avoid them. It's significant that Tarotists cannot seem to decide if the person is male or female; in sorrow we lose everything that distinguishes us.

But sorrow for what? What do the spilled Cups represent? The obvious connection will be the optimism of the *Three*. Did the women prematurely assume their new community had established itself? If so, the rest of the suit shows the struggle to put things on a firmer footing, with the *Ten* a joyous result. But maybe the sorrow goes deeper. Maybe the Cups symbolize everything lost in the collapse of the old. We cannot really begin until we come to terms with our grief.

Divinatory meanings: **Sorrow at something lost or wasted. Acceptance.**
Reversed: **The time comes to move on. We can imagine that the cloaked figure turns around, picks up the two Cups and carries them over the bridge to the small house.**
Action: **Grieve for what is lost.**

Six of Cups

Many find this card a little strange. In a cozy village a figure dressed in bright red and blue hands a Cup with flowers to a child who appears over-dressed for the Spring day. The whole thing may remind us of a fairy tale—in other words, a child's fantasy. The usual way people see this card is nostalgia, which is to say a memory of a happier time. But is it memory or fantasy? Often nostalgia glosses over the more painful aspects of past experience to create just that fairy tale fantasy of a past that never was. Danger comes when we don't realize it's a fantasy and try to avoid challenges by escaping into a past that never was.

In the idea of Cups the struggle to create a new world nostalgia can mean a look back at the old, a retreat into rosy memories after the failure shown in the Five.

Divinatory meanings: **Nostalgia, looking backwards, rosy memories.**
Reversed: **A more honest look at the past. Moving towards the future.**
Action: **A time to look back on the past rather than try to move forward.**

Seven of Cups

In the *Six* we saw the attraction, and perhaps the risk, of looking back to a vision of the past that never really was. Ironically, the way forward does not lie in sober realism but more fantasy.

A figure stands in silhouette, with his back to us and his feet unseen. In other words, he is ungrounded, undefined, and seemingly unattached to reality. He stares at seven Cups that appear in the clouds, each one containing some bizarre wonder out of a dream or a fairy tale—a floating head, a cloaked radiant figure, treasures, a dragon. But none are real.

As with the *Four* some take a moralistic approach to the card. He should get his head out of the clouds and get to work creating the world he wants. But such Puritanism misses the point. The first step to serious change begins with the ability and the freedom to imagine something different. When we can imagine we can discover possibilities.

Divinatory meanings: Fantasies, visions, the ability to imagine new possibilities.
Reversed: Action to make real a fantasy or desire.
Action: Fantasize on possibilities before taking action.

Eight of Cups

As with the *Eight of Wands* we see a turning point. A figure walks away from *eight Cups* stacked neatly in two rows. With the *Moon* shining down benignly he seems to start out on a journey or a quest. Traditionally the card means to walk away from something because we know the time has come, even if nothing has collapsed. We might compare it to the *Five*. Here no Cups lie spilled on the ground, he just leaves. Then what makes this a turning point?

Notice the odd way the artist has arranged the Cups, with a gap in the top row. They imply that something is missing, some vital piece. The suit begins with a too easy optimism, the idea that good intentions alone can re-make the world. The collapse of the *Five* gives way to nostalgia in the *Six*. The *Seven* then inspired us to imagine something new, and now the *Eight* searches to discover the true power that will create a new world.

Divinatory meanings: Leaving something behind. A quest for what is missing.
Reverse: Staying in a situation. Not a time to abandon what you have.
Action: Walk away from something before it ends. Seek what is missing.

Nine of Cups

Coming after the quest of the *Eight,* the *Nine* and the *Ten* show alternate results, each one successful in its own way. The *Ten* will give us a family, symbol of communal happiness, while the *Nine* presents a single figure, a plump man, seemingly smug and self-satisfied. A fortune-telling tradition refers to the *Nine* as the "wish card." If it appears in your reading, fate will grant your wish.

But what if your wish is just to own the most Cups? We see them all lined up on a table, no gaps as in the *Eight.* There is nothing much else in the picture, just a curtain to hide whatever may lie under the table. The position of his arms looks relaxed until we notice how his elbows stick out. Try it and you might find it stiff and defensive. The *Nines,* the last single digit number, all show someone alone, the limits of individual action. Only in the Pentacles do we find an image of fulfillment.

Divinatory meanings: A wish granted. Self-satisfaction. Smugness.
Reversed: Looking for something deeper. The quest is not over.
Action: Enjoy what you have

Ten of Cups

In one of the deck's happiest images we see fulfillment of the goal to create a new world. A man and woman raise their arms in recognition of a rainbow filled with Cups, while two children dance together in carefree joy. Beyond the family we see a simple house set among trees. Their happiness does not come from possessions, in contrast to the *Ten of Pentacles* where we see a wealthier family who appears strained and tense.

The rainbow suggests a spiritual, almost mythic quality to this culmination of the Way of the Heart. In some cultures the rainbow forms a bridge between Heaven and Earth. In the Bible we find a story similar to what we have been considering in this book. A flood destroys the world, leaving Noah and his family and the animals to start over. At the end of the great flood God sets a rainbow in the sky as a promise it will never happen again.

Divinatory meanings: Happiness, fulfillment, deep emotional bonds. Family and community.
Reversed: Strains in a family or group. Difficulty appreciating what you have.
Action: A time to celebrate and honor emotional ties, especially family.

Page of Cups

This delightful picture continues the fairy tale quality seen in a number of the Cups cards. A jaunty young man, his tunic decorated with lotus flowers, smiles as he looks at a fish who half emerges from his Cup. The fish's mouth appears open and we can imagine it actually talking to the *Page,* promising to grant him three wishes, or revealing mysteries.

The *Cups* Court cards show us a quest to bring spiritual healing of the Grail to a world moving through upheavals. The *Page* does not leave on a quest, like the *Knight,* or create, like the *Queen,* or govern, like the *King.* Instead, he provides a sense of magic and wonder. And maybe—just maybe—a magical talking fish exists, and will appear to us if we do the right thing. The idea of animal allies appears in every culture except one—the mechanistic world of industrial society. Maybe this card signifies the return of an older and deeper world.

Divinatory meanings: Fascination, magic. A young person, gentle and imaginative.
Reversed: Closing off imagination. Being told to "grow up."
Action: Be aware of magic in your life, especially omens.

Knight of Cups

The dreamy slow moving Knight holds the great quest object, the Holy Grail, container of the spiritual force that can heal the "Wasteland" and bring new life to the world. The horse seems to move through desert sands, while across the stream we see trees, as if the healing has begun. Thus, we can see this card as a promise of salvation, and the bearer of that salvation.

Except—notice how slow everything seems, without urgency. Many have found a self-absorbed quality in this *Knight.* Traditionally, Cups is the suit of love, and thus the *Knight* becomes a figure of romance. Many, however, find him too caught up in his own dreams. He holds up the Cup. Does he want to offer it, or just stare at it, fascinated? Here is a question you might ask yourself, or the questioner, when this card appears: has the *Knight* fulfilled his quest? Is he returning with the Grail? Or is he still on his journey?

Divinatory meanings: Someone on a spiritual quest. A bringer of healing. Dreamy lover.
Reversed: Conflict between inner fascination and outer attractions or responsibilities.
Action: Move slowly, be aware of feeling in the midst of action.

Queen of Cups

We can describe the Cups suit as the spiritual healing of the world, and thus from a prophetic point of view, the most significant cards in the Minor Arcana. The Cups Court cards tell their own story, a quest to find and bring back the Grail. The *Page* contemplated it, the *Knight* went in search of it, and now, it seems, he's brought it back and given it to his lady, the *Queen.*

She sits on her throne carved with cherubic mermaids, and stares at the most complex of all the Cups. It resembles the vessel which holds the "host" in the ritual of communion. Its design also recalls the Ark of the Covenant, container of the divine energy which upholds the world. Like the *Knight* she stares at it with intensity, maybe pondering the best way to use it. Though she sits on the land, the water of emotion flows into her dress.

Divinatory meanings: Someone strong and dedicated. A healer. Her intensity can be intimidating.
Reversed: She may lose her sense of service and get lost in her own emotion.
Action: Be a holder of visions.

King of Cups

The *Queen* is the heart of the Cups suit, the visionary figure whose commitment drives the magical restoration at the heart of the suit. The *King* becomes her consort, the outer figure who must take charge and run the new society on a day by day basis. Thus the *King* channels all the creative and spiritual energy of the suit into practical expression. His throne either floats on the waves (hard to imagine stone being able to do that!) or else rises above them. Either way, the water does not touch him.

Like the *Queen,* his expression appears very forceful. They form a powerful duo and strong partnership, each one aware of their great responsibility, hers to envision a new world, his to make it work. As well as a Cup he holds a scepter of power.

Divinatory meanings: A strong man, a leader, especially when partnered with a powerful woman. He may suppress his own emotional or creative side in order to act responsibly.
Reversed: He may experiment with new approaches, or seek new ways to express his inner life.
Action: A time to direct emotional or creative energy to practical uses.

Ace of Swords

Each suit presents its own part in the struggle for a new creation. Swords bring the most difficult part, the acceptance of everything we've lost. Whether the great change will come through actual destruction or more gradually, there is a level at which we resist change. The mind does not want to absorb it. And so we see figures in this suit who are blindfolded, or covering their faces, or moving away from us, their faces hidden.

At the base of the suit, however, lies the *Ace*. The strongest and most difficult of the *Aces,* this is the power of mind, but also destruction. The *yods* this time take the form of drops of light, to illuminate difficult truths. The hand appears to hold the Sword tightly, as if it's difficult to hold. Like the sword of *Justice* it points straight up, for absolute truth as it pierces through the crown of earthly power to something greater.

Divinatory meanings: Truth, illumination, a calm mind in the face of difficulties.
Reversed: Resistance to truth. A commitment wavers. Possibly fanaticism.
Action: Think very clearly, uninfluenced by emotion or desire.

Two of Swords

Commitment to painful truth can be a burden, and so we see someone who has retreated into isolation and denial. She has blindfolded herself and now holds her Swords like a barrier to anyone—or any reality—that might try to approach her. Holding the Swords that way blocks her heart and lungs, and raises her center of gravity, so that ironically someone who comes close without making noise could tip her over into the rough water. Denial is a dangerous state. This holds true on the personal level as well as the larger one, for if we refuse to look at our problems they can hurt us all the more.

We can find a more positive view if we consider her posture a meditative state. Then we might say she has closed off outer stimulation, including people, so that she can send her attention inwards. In such a state she may become an oracle, a speaker of prophecy.

Divinatory meanings: Denial, closing off from others. Alternatively, a deep inner state, prophecy.
Reversed: Knocked over, disturbed, roused from a deep inner state.
Action: A time to separate from others, turn your awareness inwards.

Three of Swords

In the *Three of Cups* people rejoiced together in a premature celebration of a renewed world. Here we see no people, but the three Swords through a single heart implies people who suffer together, who share their sorrow at all that's been lost. As with the violent images throughout the suit it does not matter if the card refers to actual disasters or just upheavals of change that may feel like a world has died.

And just as the joy in the Cups turned out to be premature, with struggles and journeys to come, so the seeming acceptance in this card will weaken, as people become isolated, or don't want to see what has happened. The fact that we see no actual people, only the universal symbol of emotion (an actual heart looks nothing like this) gives the card a kind of purity. Like the *Ace* it rises above individual personality.

Divinatory meanings: Compassion, sadness, acceptance of sorrow.
Reversed: Difficulty accepting an unpleasant truth. Conflict between people who should be supporting each other in a difficult time
Action: Allow suffering into your heart, grieve for what is lost.

Four of Swords

One of the stranger cards in the suit, it invites several interpretations. Most see it as rest or withdrawal, as if a knight has gone to a chapel and now sleeps peacefully. Or is that really asleep? An odd light suffuses his body, as if he's entered an altered state. Is he meditating? The hands come together in a gesture of prayer, probably impossible to hold for someone sleeping.

Could he be in a coma and placed there in hopes of a magical cure? The stained glass window seems to show Christ or a saint blessing—or healing—a disciple. The word *Pax*, Latin for "peace," appears in a halo above Christ's head. The knight may signify more than just an individual. He may symbolize the wounded world itself. The Grail legends tell of a wounded "Fisher King" whose body lies at the center of the Wasteland. Both the king and the land cannot heal, or awaken, by themselves, but only through the sacred power of the Grail.

Divinatory meanings: Withdrawal, rest, retreat to an inner state. A need for healing.
Reversed: Arousal, return to action. Connection to others.
Action: Retreat from battle. Find a place to rest and heal.

Five of Swords

Some people see the prominent red-haired man and assume the card signifies some great triumph, or at least confidence. However, Pamela Smith drew this picture to illustrate the concept of defeat. Thus, we can focus on the two smaller figures who, like so many, turn their backs on us and walk away.

The "defeat" here can refer to the losses and breakdowns of the old structures, but also the collapse of the attempt in the *Three* (there are three figures here) to unite people in shared suffering. Rather than truth, the Swords here symbolize conflict, possibly even destruction. The water is choppy, the skies jagged with clouds, the world a mirror of our inner state. Some see the two smaller figures as different reactions to defeat. Both have lost their Swords and become powerless, but the one nearest the water covers his face in shame or despair, while the one closer to us holds his head up and walks away.

Divinatory meanings: Defeat, dejection, feelings of weakness or shame.
Reversed: Looking beyond loss or defeat. Recovery.
Action: Something cannot be overcome. Accept defeat and walk away.

Six of Swords

The original book for this deck, by Waite, gives the meanings for this card as "Journey by water; route; envoy." Most people find something deeper in the mysterious picture. A woman and a child sit huddled in a shallow boat, the woman bent over and cloaked, the child tight against her side. Behind them, a man with a black pole, like the *Fool's* stick, pushes the boat through the still waters to an island in the distance. Everything is silent, subdued.

Who are these people? Refugees from a dying world? Do they seek sanctuary? Are the Swords they carry, upright as if stuck in the boat, memories of what they've lost? There is another, more mythic possibility. In Greek myth a ferryman named Charon carried the dead in such a boat, from the living world to the next one. Are they literally dead, victims of a collapsing world? Maybe they represent the painful transition, conscious of what was lost, not yet in the new.

Divinatory meanings: Sad memories. Difficulty letting go of the past.
Reversed: Attempts to release the past and begin again. Breaking a silence.
Action: A time to protect others, to travel with them if necessary.

Seven of Swords

Again we find a figure looking backwards, at the same time that he moves forward. A man who appears pleased with himself tiptoes away from a tent, carrying five Swords over his shoulders. Two remain standing, as if he cannot take them all, but he doesn't seem to mind. We might think of him as the great hero of mythologies the world over, the trickster thief.

He suggests to us an approach to crises that tackles nothing head on but rather finds creative ways around opposition. In radical times such figures can become folk heroes, like Robin Hood, or the bank robbers of the 1930s.

At the same time, such attitudes do not really solve problems or create anything new. This is why he looks backward, and why as pleased with himself as he is, he has not really changed the situation. He raises questions of effectiveness but also ethics. For if it's *your* Swords he's stealing he can become destructive.

Divinatory meanings: Someone sly and tricky who acts on his own.
Reversed: Seeking joint effort for more serious change.
Action: Subtle action is necessary. Do something tricky.

Eight of Swords

In the *Eight of Wands* and the *Eight of Cups* we saw hints of a break-through. Here we see what looks like the opposite, a literal bondage that implies helplessness, confusion, ignorance. In the *Two* the woman chooses her blindfold, for if she wanted she could set down the Swords and take it off. But you can't tie yourself up like this woman, someone else has to do it. Behind her we see a gray castle, symbol maybe of the power of the old world that tries to stop the new from emerging.

But look—the ropes do not go around her legs, and the Swords do not block her way, and there is no one there from the castle. What stops her is the blind-fold—confusion and fear.

As with the *Two* there is another possibility. Maybe our intellects cannot see a clear path. Maybe all we can do is move forward blindly, trusting our instincts.

Divinatory meanings: Ignorance, confusion, possibly imposed by others. Move forward one step at a time.
Reversed: Seeing things clearly. First steps towards liberation.
Action: A moment when you cannot see beyond your immediate limitations. Small steps.

Nine of Swords

Throughout this suit we have seen people blindfolded, huddled, looking backwards, turning away, as the suit develops the theme of how hard it can be to accept the death of the old world. Here we see another such figure, a woman who sits up in bed and covers her face with her hands. On the surface it seems as strong a denial as the *Two*.

And yet, there is something going on here, a prelude to acceptance. For after all, she has awoken. The coma of the *Four* is over. One of only two cards in the deck with a black background—the other is the Devil—the *Eight* embodies the famous Dark Night of the Soul, when we awaken to a terrible truth. Behind her the Swords form a painful ladder of truth.

The comforter on the bed indeed gives images of consolation. Red roses, for passion, alternate with the signs of the zodiac, as if the universe would protect her as she climbs out of despair.

Divinatory meanings: Painful truth, sadness. The need to face something.
Reversed: Beginning the process of climbing out of despair.
Action: A time of deep sorrow that must be acknowledged.

Ten of Swords

At first glance this appears the most dire of all the Swords cards, perhaps the entire deck. Even the *Death* card appears more hopeful. And even though dead he seems to look the other way, still unable to face the truth. So one way we might view this card is to say that if we never find a way to accept the end of the old world, if we keep to denial, it will destroy us.

And yet, the card contains something deeper. For one thing, the black night of the *Nine* is lifting as a golden dawn appears beyond the calm waters. The man's face turns away from us but towards that light. And notice the fingers—they form the priestly blessing of the *Hierophant*. So maybe the picture, with its extreme violence at the end of the suit shows an acceptance—even if forced upon us—that will finally release the past and allow the birth of a future.

Divinatory meanings: Mental distress, often exaggerated. Resistance to change worsens a situation.
Reversed: An extreme situation clears the way for something new.
Action: An extreme situation is already beginning to change.

Page of Swords

The Swords' Court cards show the struggle to direct mental energy to productive purpose. The mind can turn negative when it sees every possibility. In general, the Courts are figures of ever increasing responsibility, from the (mostly) carefree *Pages,* to the active *Knights,* to the ruling *Queens* and *Kings.* This becomes a special problem for the suit of Mind, the most unfocused of the elements. The *Page* shows this difficulty of focus by moving forwards while facing backwards, as if, like so many of the numbered *Swords* cards, he cannot let go of the past.

At the same time, *Pages* carry the least responsibility of the four Courts, and so we see him standing lightly, and yet alert as he holds up his Sword. As the old expression goes, his head is in the clouds, unconnected to daily life. Maybe he looks back to his last day of freedom, before he must become a *Knight.*

*Divinatory meanings: **Wariness, alertness. Looking back to the past while moving forward.***

*Reversed: **Be careful of trickery, or a buildup of tension.***

*Action: **Caution. Look behind you as you move forward.***

Knight of Swords

A heroic figure charges forward, visor up so we can see his fierce expression. He raises his Sword high above his head, tilted forward in a commitment to aggressive action. This is the only horse that gallops, the way a *Knight's* steed is meant to do. The trees on the left bend towards him, which means he is charging into a storm. The horse seems to look back at him, as if it questions his recklessness, but it obeys its master's command. The horse symbolizes the animal instinct of survival, the *Knight* the heroic consciousness that overrides all doubt.

Waite, the deck's designer, referred to him as Sir Galahad, the image of the knightly ideal of courage and dedication. And yet, he appears focused on battle and swift action, lacking Cups' inner vision, or Wands' love of adventure for its own sake, or Pentacles' steady devotion. Creating a new world requires courage and a willingness to fight all the enemies of the new community, but other qualities are necessary as well.

*Divinatory meanings: **Courage, heroism, single-mindedness, possible recklessness.***

*Reversed: **Doubt, fear, but also caution.***

*Action: **A time for courage and swift movement. Do not hesitate.***

Queen of Swords

More than any other card in the suit, the *Queen* returns us to the purity of the *Ace*. Her perfectly upright Sword, like that of the Ace, but also *Justice*, shows a commitment to truth above all else. Unlike the *King*, who must make decisions and rule, she dedicates herself to taking on the suffering of the world. This is the meaning of her open left hand, that she will hold others' pain as a world ends. The tassel around her wrist resembles the "widow's cord" worn by women in Victorian England. She does not mourn a personal loss so much as all those who have suffered in the hard times.

The *Queen of Cups* holds the vision of new creation. *The Queen of Swords* holds the sorrow of loss. And yet, she looks to the future, not the past, for she faces right, the direction of manifestation, while her crown of golden butterflies symbolizes transformation.

Divinatory meanings: **Sorrow, but also wisdom and hope. Idealism and clear vision.**
Reversed: **Turning away from clarity, danger of personal bias.**
Action: **Speak the truth with total commitment.**

King of Swords

Like *Justice* in the Major Arcana he looks right at us, the only Court card to do so. He challenges us to do the right thing, to act on principle, to be a force for *Justice*. Unlike the *Queen,* his Sword does not point straight up. This does not signify confusion or corruption (though that might come in the reversed position) but rather his responsibility to make decisions and enforce laws, for he is the head of government, a position intellectual Swords takes very seriously. Thus, he holds a dual purpose, symbolized by two birds behind him (as compared to the *Queen,* who is more single-minded). His first, and most over-riding purpose is principle. All his authority means nothing without it. The second is practicality, the ability to lead successfully. He is the most practical of the *Kings* but also the most dedicated.

As with the *Queen,* butterflies adorn his crown and his high austere throne. His true dedication is to transform the world.

Divinatory meanings: **Authority, power, decision-making, but also emotional distance. Responsibility.**
Reversed: **Power leads to temptation, possibly corruption.**
Action: **Accept the responsibility of making decisions for others.**

Ace of Pentacles

The first thing we might notice is that there are no *yods,* no leaves, drops of water, or light. This does not make this *Ace* less spiritual, or less of a gift. We still see a white hand emerge from a cloud. But this is the gift of Earth, of solid reality. In Pentacles we see the task and the promise of putting together a world. Wands gave us life energy, Cups vision, Swords the mind coming to terms with pathetic truth. Pentacles makes it possible to go beyond all that and fulfill the prophecy.

At the same time we should remember that the Pentacle itself—a five pointed star in a circle filled with golden light—is a symbol of magic, the human body as a link between Heaven and Earth. Our new world must never forget the spirit power that makes it all possible.

Divinatory meanings: A good start to a project. Offers of money or work.

Reversed: Can be a false start, or hardship. May indicate going beyond the practical to explore new possibilities.

Action: A moment of lushness and abundance. Accept an offer.

Two of Pentacles

A lively young man seems to dance or play with a pair of Pentacles in a ribbon shaped like the infinity sign. Behind him a pair of ships ride the waves of a rolling sea. How we see the meaning depends on how we read the card's mood. Does he seem to be having fun? We might view the sea as stormy, but also cartoon-like. Does he lightly juggle the Pentacles or is he having trouble holding them? To put it another way, are they light or heavy? Do you see his face as playful or anxious?

The *Ace* gave us single-minded purpose but here the practical work begins. We need to balance or juggle different needs and obligations. Do we do it with grace or anxiety? The infinity sign links him to the *Magician* and *Strength*—or maybe his responsibilities seem endless.

Divinatory meanings: Juggling or balancing different tasks and responsibilities. Can we do them playfully or do they become a burden?

Reversed: Dropping something, either deliberately or because it becomes a burden.

Action: Juggle different priorities with a playful air.

Three of Pentacles

The *Threes* show scenes of early success, in which the goal of the suit appears well on its way. In *Wands* a strong figure sends out ships, in Cups people celebrate as if the new world already exists, and in Swords we seem to accept the sorrow of all that has been lost. In each case the early success falls apart, with the real work to come. So it is here. The goal of people working together to create a new and spiritually meaningful world appears well underway. But problems will soon follow.

A sculptor stands on a bench, his mallet (an actual medieval tool) ready to strike. Before acting, however, he turns towards a monk and a man who holds the plans of the church. The spiritual and the practical support the work of creating something new and beautiful. Despite the medieval and Christian setting we can view this as an ideal for people working together to build a new world.

Divinatory meanings: Work at a high level. Cooperation, support from others.
Reversed: Acting alone. Conflict between people who should work together.
Action: A time to cooperate with others in work at the highest level.

Four of Pentacles

In this card and the next we see the breakdown of the ideal shown in the *Three*. There are subtle ways to interpret the Four and *Five*, but it's hard to escape the idea that greed and power interfere with the creation of community. Here a king seems to gather all the Pentacles, and if we remember that people originally called this suit Coins we realize that the old inequalities of wealth reassert themselves. There are only two crowned figures in the deck who are not official *Kings, Queens,* or the *Empress* and *Emperor.* These are the dead king on the *Death* card, and the *Four of Pentacles.* Thus what the Death card seemed to sweep away appears to come back.

He does not just hoard the Pentacles, he uses them as shields, one under each foot, as if the Earth might overwhelm him from Below, one on his head to block spiritual power from Above, and one on his chest to cover his heart and lungs.

Divinatory meanings: Hoarding, inequality. Using wealth or power to cut oneself off from life.
Reversed: The shield comes down, he seeks another way, or life overwhelms him.
Action: Hold on tightly to what you have.

Five of Pentacles

Here we see the other side of the inequality introduced in the *Four*. It's significant that we see them outside a church, first because a place of sanctuary seems to have shut them out—many people have noticed that the picture shows a stained glass window but no door—but also because the *Three's* vision of shared effort took place *inside* a church.

All the *Fives* show life's challenges but this is one of the hardest, for the realm of Pentacles is that of money and the body. Do you see the bell around the man's neck? In medieval times people with Hansen's Disease—so-called "lepers"—were mistakenly thought to be so contagious that they had to wear bells to warn people to stay away. Thus the picture represents not just suffering but the return of ancient prejudices. We seem to have fallen far from the promise of the *Ace!*

Divinatory meanings: Hardship, suffering, feeling shut out, possibly because of prejudice. People, especially outsiders, supporting each other in hard times.

Reversed: A situation improves. People's bonds may weaken as physical conditions get better.

Action: A time to support each other when institutions and authority won't help.

Six of Pentacles

A man "in the guise of a merchant," as Waite described him, gives coins to a beggar while another waits for his turn. Though the two on their knees are clearly not the same pair as on the *Five* a line runs between the two cards. We have seen how the *Sixes* bring order or restore optimism after the breakdowns of the *Fives*—leadership in Wands, kindness in Cups, leaving defeat behind in Swords. Here we see an antidote to the *Four* and *Five of Pentacles*.

And yet, charity can be limited as a response to suffering. Many people have pointed out that the two have to beg on their knees, while the merchant seems to measure out the coins. The balanced scales, however, point to something much deeper than counting coins. They evoke *Justice,* the pivotal card of the Major Arcana. *Justice* is vital here, for without it all our practical steps will just recreate the old world.

Divinatory meanings: Kindness, charity, someone who acts in a just way. Asking for help.

Reversed: Someone who acts unjustly. Or, people who no longer need help.

Action: Give or accept something of value.

Seven of Pentacles

As if the *Six* resolves the crisis triggered by the *Four* and *Five,* we see a much simpler image, with the theme of work. The suit will now move steadily towards its goal of a new and functioning society. The first stage of the process is the willingness to work for it. The Pentacle offered in the *Ace* has become a seed buried in the ground, and now a bush with seven Pentacles grows lushly as the gardener looks on. The magic from Above has truly taken root below.

More even than with most other cards we need to ask the questioner (or ourselves) about his expression. Does he appear satisfied with what he has done? Is he now taking a well-earned rest? Or does he stare, dismayed, at everything he still needs to do? The answer determines how we understand the message, either in a personal reading, or on the larger scale of world change.

Divinatory meanings: Hard work that makes something grow. Magic taking root in daily life.
Reversed: Return to work. Service to the Earth.
Action: A moment to step back and consider what you've done.

Eight of Pentacles

The theme of work continues, even more settled than in the *Seven*. The figure here works on one Pentacle after another, calm, dedicated. Notice they all appear slightly different. We can say he's learning, or that he's an artisan, not a machine. Does this imply that the new world will return to more individual work?

In the *Three* we saw a premature vision of groups working together in a spiritual setting. Here we see the practical steps to make vision a reality. It's the work that matters, not the result, or the money, or recognition. Though we see a road leading to a city no one is there, either to buy his Pentacles or to admire them.

The *Eights* all show progress. Wands bring energies together, in Cups people seek what is missing. Even the helpless *Eight of Swords* contains hints of change. This *Eight* is the simplest, the most rooted and the clearest. Unlike the others, he does not need to leave to move towards the goal.

Divinatory meanings: Work, dedication, learning a skill.
Reversed: Impatience or procrastination. Loss of focus in work.
Action: A time to work steadily, without concern for reward or recognition.

Nine of Pentacles

As with the other suits the final single digit number, which is the number of months of pregnancy, shows us an image of completion of the journey before the more concrete established situation of the *Ten*. Here we return to the image we saw in the *Seven,* the Pentacles growing on the bush. The magic sign that unites Heaven and Earth has taken root, and now clusters of grapes also grow on the bushes, an image of lush abundance. The flower designs on her dress resemble the woman/Venus symbol on the *Empress's* shield, hinting that the Goddess of the Earth has come to life to bless the transformed world.

Notice the trained falcon on her wrist. The hood puts him under her control but he will fly very high when she releases him, only to return to her control. He symbolizes the trained and disciplined mind. Discipline even more than work holds the key to this card's transformation creative energy.

Divinatory meanings: Success through discipline and training. Satisfaction. Achievement.
Reversed: Isolation. Loss of discipline or concern more with relationship.
Action: Discipline will bring great rewards.

Ten of Pentacles

Here we see the conclusion of the effort to create a stable—and wealthy—society. We see a family in either an ordered town or their own manor courtyard. Well dressed, prosperous, they appear in sharp contrast to the simple family and setting of the *Ten of Cups.* But where that family celebrated joyously these people seem tense, the man looking away from the woman, the child clinging to his mother's dress and holding on to the dog. They may have developed the practical side of Pentacles but forgotten the magical.

And yet, the magic is all around them. The *ten Pentacles* form a famous Kabbalistic diagram known as the Tree of Life. Other cards hint at it, but this is the only place it appears in full. But while in virtually every other card the people and the symbols interact, here they just overlay the picture. Most significantly, a mysterious old man, symbol of the spiritual world, sits just outside the archway. Only the dogs notice him.

Divinatory meanings: Wealth, stability, security. Possible lack of emotion.
Reversed: Venturing outside one's safe world into the unknown.
Action: Enjoy your surroundings but recognize there is more to your world than what you see.

Page of Pentacles

He walks slowly through green fields, his Pentacle held up before him. If we put this card together with the *Ace* we can imagine a sort of fairy tale in which a poor young man sees a ghostly hand offer him a magic star that will heal the world after a cataclysm. Where will he go with it, and how will he use it?

The energy is strong, and as a young *Page* he has to hold it on his fingertips. Because Pentacles represent the Earth, and such issues as work and money, sometimes we think of them as dull. But this card reminds us that ultimately the Pentacle is the strongest, most mystical, of all the tools on the *Magician's* table. In traditional fortune telling the *Pages* are messengers. This *Page* brings the message of restoration and magic.

Pages also are called the students, and here we see the model of someone fascinated by what he studies, with no concern for practical matters beyond his subject.

Divinatory meanings: Fascination, hope. A dedicated student, especially of magic.
Reversed: Distractions, loss of purpose or belief, confusion.
Action: Immerse yourself in something that fascinates you.

Knight of Pentacles

He is the only *Knight* whose horse does not move. The Wands horse rears up, Cups goes slowly, as in a dream, Swords gallops but this black steed stands in place, head up, alert, but unmoving on a small hilltop. Beyond them lie the plowed fields of the new community.

Modern Tarot tradition usually sees him as hard-working, dedicated, and maybe a bit dull, the sort who won't take a vacation because he'd fall too far behind. But if we see the Pentacles as the creation of a new world, one that will endure and become stable, then the *Knight* becomes its perfect guardian. The fact that he doesn't ride off seeking battles or dragons to slay, does not look for romance with a fair lady, means that people can count on him. We might imagine a community grown up around him, forgetting almost that he is there, but safe because his Pentacle protects them.

Divinatory meanings: Dedicated, hard-working, a protector, someone to be counted on.
Reversed: Someone who questions his dedication, or decides to try something new.
Action: A time to work steadily. Quietly protect those around you.

Queen of Pentacles

All the *Queens* hold the deep energy of the suit, Wands its life energy, Cups its vision, Swords its sorrow. With Pentacles showing such an emphasis on practicality and development of a stable society the *Queen* holds a vital connection to nature and to magic. The two combine in awareness of the wonder of existence, exactly the quality that can get lost as the world settles down to a new reality.

She sits on a throne in nature, removed from any city or royal castle, or even the cultivated farmlands of the *Knight*. At lower right we see a brown rabbit, symbol of fertility. The leaves over her like a bower may remind us of the *Magician*, and in fact she wears his colors, red over white. The *Magician* is the second card (after the *Fool*), and the *Queen* comes next to last, so the two form a circle of magic. She looks in her Pentacle as in a crystal ball. She may be a seer.

Divinatory meanings: Lover of nature, sense of the magic of daily life. Possibly a seer or a witch.

Reversed: More involved with people, social structures, communal activites.

Action: A time to go deeply into your love of nature.

King of Pentacles

The *Fool* began the deck as a free wanderer, unattached to property or responsibility. At the other end of the deck we find the grand *King of Pentacles,* wealthy, secure, in charge of a settled world. Though he sits in front of a stone wall, with his castle rising up behind him, nature grows wildly around him. Flowers poke out from his crown, leaves and vines are everywhere, and grape clusters seem to hang on his robe. He also seems the most comfortable of all the *Kings,* at ease on his throne as he fondly touches the Pentacle on his knee.

Bulls heads appear on the corners of his throne, symbol of Taurus, the "fixed" sign of Earth and thus the most stable and grounded of all the signs. The throne is black, like fertile ground. Here at the end of the deck—the end of the prophecy—we find stability, the world restored after the great upheavals, but also lush and filled with life.

Divinatory meanings: Wealth, stability, satisfaction. A benevolent ruler (boss).

Reversed: His comfort becomes uppermost, more important than his responsibilities to others.

Action: Express your satisfaction with possessions and the good things in life.

Queen of Pentacles • King of Pentacles

12 Months / 36 Decans

The Qualities of Time

Astrology divides each month into three sections of around ten days each. These sections are called decans (from the Greek *deka*, ten) and were already in use in the ancient world. Today, they still guide us through the year in 36 steps, and provide each phase with a distinct meaning.

The Order of the Golden Dawn, an important English Rosicrucian society around 1900, which played a pivotal role in the history of Tarot, was the first to establish a systematic connection between astrology and Tarot (cf. Israel Regardie [ed.], *The Complete Golden Dawn System of Magic*. Various editions.).

In doing so, each sign of the zodiac was associated with six cards in total, and each decan with one particular Tarot card. These attributions of the Order of the Golden Dawn were used in the decks of A.E. Waite and A. Crowley: Crowley has noted the decans on his cards, and Waite often depicts them on his images, for example by showing bull's heads on the *King of Pentacles* or the sign of Aries on the *The Emperor*. You will find exactly these correspondences on the following pages.

When you live in harmony with the yearly cycle, you return to certain tasks and revelations each year. Our spirit matures and consolidates, like a tree gaining its annual rings, and gradually grounds itself deep in the earth and grows skywards to heaven.

Turning a Desert into a Garden

The Aries Month
(21 March – 20 April)

The beginning of spring marks the beginning of a new seasonal cycle. It is an advantageous time for starting new projects. Thus, the Aries month represents the principle of a new *start*, it means that you know how to use and *start* your life. *"I am"* defines this sign, Fire is its element.

IV-The Emperor

The powers of self-determination, the task to rule one's life. In Christianity (and other religions) Easter is the highest festival. In Germany, bonfires are lit on Easter eve, and they spell the message that "life will conquer death ... and what once was desert will turn into a garden." This is what the image of the Emperor is meant to say. In a positive sense, the golden apples and the *Crux ansata* in his right hand indicate that emperors possess great fertility and will be

Life conquers death

THE EMPEROR

THE TOWER

Learn to love and fly – or violence and destruction

Mistress of our love and our urges

QUEEN of WANDS

pioneers in reclaiming the stony desert as arable land (in a negative sense the card warns against stubbornness and power politics which petrify and waste the greatest fertility).

XVI-The Tower

Two archetypes inform this image's content: *The Tower of Babel* represents this picture's destructive aspect. *Pentecost*, when the Holy Spirit came down in the form of tongues of fire, is the positive aspect of this card. It deals with our highest energies (depicted by the flash of lightning). By force we may destroy. By love we may abandon our ivory tower, our loneliness and aloofness and risk a jump into life. In a positive sense, we are here talking about letting ourselves fall—and learning to fly!

Queen of Wands

With her black cat and the sunflowers she is the mistress of our highest energies, she knows how to direct—and to enjoy—our urges and our love. Again, we here have the motive of a desert turned into a garden!

21 March – 20 April

A time of beginning

Two Wands

1st decan of Aries (21 – 31 March)

Lust and burden of beginnings: the art of using people, tasks, and energies for a start. This card describes the great power you need and gain when you pace your energy carefully.

The Wands mean driving force, zest for action, will power and self-development. Two Wands mean polarities which may either block each other, or strengthen each other. How do you deal with conflicting urges and ambitions—with instincts and aims which are disputed by your own self or between you and others? Conflicting urges and a clash of interests have to be handled carefully, especially in a partnership. It is less a thing of arguments, rather of consideration and action. Whoever forgets one of the Wands will produce only part work (and fails). Whoever solves conflicts by individually processing part by part will gain something whole.

Don't be forced into a quandary. Do not do things by halves. The questions you are facing right now enable you to discover your power, your specific outlook (the globe in the figure's hand). Something new is developing, and only you can discover it. Reply to rudeness with rudeness. Now it's up to you.

Advice ➤ **Wait until your point of view is completed and you know exactly what to do. Then hesitate no more! Act with all your might. Your success depends on your undiminished will and enthusiasm.**

21 – 31 March

A time of sober-mindedness

2nd decan of Aries (1 – 10 April)

Three Wands

You are a powerful, rooted person. Your wealth in ideas, energy and drive combines with your love of adventure and your willingness to change things. This card stands for solid work, and for the many objectives before you, and for your delight in starting things.

It may tell you to wait no longer. There is nothing you must be afraid of. Start right now! An idea is only worth what you make of it. Look ahead. You can rely on your strength and the integrity of your intentions. Go ahead to new horizons.

The opportunities of this sunny and fiery phase of the yearly cycle depend on discerning or ignoring your darker sides. This is the only picture which shows a yellow sky with a grey tone behind: the unconscious plays a role. To avoid feelings of aimlessness or helplessness ("rebels without a cause") you need to live consciously and watch out for the darker sides (of yourself as well as other people, events etc.)— exemplified by the back of the image's figure.

Now is a perfect time for bringing color into everyday life and light into the unexplored. Other people will approach you full of energy. But take your time. Consider carefully what is happening. "If you know what you are doing, you can do what you want." *(Moshé Feldenkrais)*.

Stay patient and firm in what you want. Don't be constrained by obstacles—let them stipulate you! ◄ *Advice*

A time of high energy

Four Wands

3rd decan of Aries (11 – 20 April)

An exhilarated attitude to life, celebration, the dance of life—full of energy, flourishing, cheering and uplifting. Yet also: we have no other image in which people are pictured as small as in this one. The danger of missing out or becoming marginalized is nowhere as imminent as here.

You can find much more than a "place of power" in wild landscapes or at specific magical sites. We are principally surrounded by the wonders of creation all the time, they root and crown our most intimate moments and experiences. Birth, wedding and death lead us to limits—and into the center of our very existence.

And through these experiences which sometimes are frightening, often wonderful, but always amazing the need for cultural activity grows—the drive to express or overcome what moves us through play, music, and dance! Celebrations and cultural events give us wings or they distract us so much we can hardly find ourselves gain. It all depends on feeling (again) what inspires us inside, and—the higher we fly—to deepen our understanding of who we are.

Be the woman or the man that you really are. Your sexual identity is an indispensable source of power.

Advice ➢ *Don't accept any rotten compromise. Avoid nitpicking solutions. Do not hide your true reasons and your authentic feelings. They offer the best motivation and guarantee beautiful results!*

Be at home in both worlds

The Taurus Month
(21 April – 21 May)

The sign of Taurus deals with continuous, purposeful work, with the dignity and the fruits of all labor (May festivities on the 1st of May). It is also a time of pleasure, of fresh growth, and new forces of life, the worship of the great Goddess and of Mother Earth (Beltane on April 30). Sense and senses awaken and aim to grow and prosper.

V-The Hierophant (High Priest)

The Hierophant is a builder of bridges (the Catholic Church still calls the Pope the *Pontifex maximus,* superior builder of bridges). He connects heaven and earth. The card either signifies the head or High Priest of the Church or confession you belong to, and / or this character stands for the priest within you. We are all called to develop and practice our own rites and traditions for the major and minor secrets of life.

21 April – 21 May

Builder of bridges and
leading figure

THE HIEROPHANT

THE EMPRESS

*Naturalness and taking
yourself for granted*

Work and earnings
from effort

KING of PENTACLES

III-The Empress

Sometimes this card indicates first of all a confrontation with the women in your life or with your own role as a woman. It deals with the unfolding of your own nature and character, with being natural. That means, your own self-image and your right to be spontaneous. It is a simple but rather very important fact that everybody is the Queen and Empress of their own life. To render this inalienable nature, this very own world fertile is what is at stake here.

King of Pentacles

The grapes indicate the hard work in the vineyard as well as the earnings from this effort (the wine which gives wings to both senses and sense—*in vino veritas,* in wine there is truth,). Taken that way, this King is a paradigm for work, sense and pleasure. "I have" defines Taurus. Its element is the Earth.

A time of cooperation

1st decan of Taurus
(21 – 30 April)

Five Pentacles

Poverty, suffering, coldness and hardship are in evidence here—or the cancelation of all these! This card deals with the ability to discover one's own needs, and to overturn a misery. It shows the story of the blind and the lame who journey together. The blind can support the lame; the lame can lead the blind. In sharing their misery, each one is redeemed from the helplessness of his situation.

Each human asset, whether possessions or talents, is only of value to the extent that it helps reduce avoidable suffering and makes unavoidable situations worth living. Some plights are the result of catastrophes and disease, and other needs which grow from unfulfilled desires such as a longing for meaning, a thirst for love, a yearning to be at home. In those situations where the fill of your possibilities connects to the mitigation of urgent needs your talents help the most!

Trust the blessing of cooperation. Help to make the world—your ≺ *Advice world—a little more human, comfortable, and convenient. Be considerate of the different rates of development. Do not measure the unequal with the equal! Take your responsibilities but do not get entangled in nonproductive dependencies or painful obligations. Start by accepting your own needs. Ask for help and help others. Together is better. Expand your ability to do good unto you and others.*

21 – 30 April

A time of gaining

Six Pentacles

2nd *decan of Taurus*
(1 – 10 May)

I f giving and taking are in equal parts, either *nothing* essential happens, as the scales don't tip because the exchange has no importance and no weight, or the scales remain balanced because *all* parties concerned actually gain something.

All good things do not come from above but from yourself. Your inner balance is what matters. You create an atmosphere of intimacy and exchange in which the differences between large and small, powerful and weak diminish. It is a situation in which you are allowed to be weak without provoking forceful reactions in others (and vice versa), after all, a situation in which you can give and take without falling on your knees or having qualms.

The joy of giving: not the charity giving away of things you do no longer need, or the misty-eyed self-abandonment in the pretended service of a good cause or idea; but offering your own ability, your concept of what would be beautiful and good; to take seriously your dreams and to actually work toward making them real. In this sense you only own what you give away, what you do not keep for and to yourself.

Advice ➤ *If you satisfy the needs with your talents; and your needs awaken and promote talents, there will only be gain. This osmosis, this productivity, is the key to the questions you have right now. Take care not to handle just the shortages, but to gain something.*

A time of significance

3rd decan of Taurus
(11 – 21 May)

Seven Pentacles

It does not matter if there is a mountain of work waiting for you or which you have just finished: here we are dealing with the stock taking of what you have already done, and with finding new objectives. Are you satisfied with what you have achieved? With the way you have worked? Your achievements mirror your life. You will see that an emotional or mental clarity is only worth what results from it, and also that your achievements and products bring only happiness and satisfaction when they express yourself.

Use this time of reflection to pinpoint what is essential for you. You will only achieve results that are worth the effort when you deal with the conventional assessments and find your own criteria. There are certain mysteries in life, and factual tasks which you will only solve the very moment in which you discover *your own* importance, your personal meaning, your task in life. Each task solved will show you that you are on your right way, and even *failure* is important when it can show you what is *not* your task or purpose.

Deal lovingly but critically with conventional criteria. You need to ◅ *Advice*
detect traces and read the signs. Each fact tells a story and conveys a message which may well be worth the effort to be studied and interpreted. This is also about your own meaning and purpose, about where you stand right now and how to act!

A time of flowering and scents

The Gemini Month (22 May – 21 June)

The month of roses is a time of plenty and completes spring. It is also the month of flowers and scents: the perfume—the diversity, the volatile stuff, but also the essence—of the spirit! "I think" defines the Gemini; their element is the Air.

This part of the yearly cycle is ruled by love and awareness. Christianity celebrates Pentecost (from "pentekoste," Greek: the fiftieth day—after Easter). The Pentecost story narrates how the Holy Spirit descends upon Christ's disciples in the form of a tongue of fire. They begin to preach and teach, and they are understood by all, no matter what their mother tongue is. Filled by the Holy Spirit, there are no longer barriers between languages, and there are no limits to understanding between individuals!

VI-The Lovers

The card of paradise, where we all once lived and which we all have lost, but which we can regain! "A marvelous living, side-by-side,

We can always regain paradise

THE LOVERS

THE MAGICIAN

Individuality and uniqueness

Weapons of the mind or a great lover

KNIGHT of SWORDS

can grow up for all people, if they succeed in loving the expanse between them, which gives them the possibility of always seeing each other as a whole and before an immense sky" *(Rainer Maria Rilke).*

I-The Magician

The magic of individuality, of you being one-of-a-kind! You are unique (cf. the figure 1). Love between all of us men and women grows and develops the more the *specialness* of each one involved is realized.

Knight of Swords

The weapons of the spirit advance tempestuously. Either thoughts running wild, restlessness, or a lack of contact to your own needs (blind zeal, driving the wrong way up the road). Or an enlightened thinker, a great lover—consistent, radical, quiet and conscious, at home in constant movement and change.

22 May – 21 June

A time of expanding consciousness

Eight Swords

1ˢᵗ decan of Gemini (22 – 31 May)

Y ou stand here bound and surrounded by swords. This shows mental prejudice, entanglement, and remote control; and / or: inner contemplation, an expanding consciousness which goes far beyond the superficial (beyond appearance and the concrete and the comprehensible). You understand the connection between thoughts (head) and actions (hands).

Just look inside and let go the common and former judgments. Inside you there is rounded, solid, ripe knowledge. You only have to be open to it. "There are thoughts you will never comprehend unless you change your life." *(Werner Sprenger).*

If you feel trapped or timid, this card tells you: there are swords at your disposal, with them you may cut off unreasonable inhibitions or addictions. Approach the swords carefully and cut away the bonds.

Unfit convictions are an obstacle; fitting convictions liberate and strengthen when we are really bound by them! In a positive sense this card demands special consequences, literally being completely *binding* in all that you are and do. Walk the talk! Learn to accept personal limitations and end mental barriers.

Advice ➤ *In your present situation, neither appearances nor customary action nor an instinctive will can be of any help. Just understand what a cornucopia of mental talents you were given.*

A time of awakening

2nd decan of Gemini
(1 – 10 June)

Nine Swords

A complete mental horizon gets dark and gloomy—or opens up freshly! Something dawns on you. When you penetrate something that was completely unexplored previously, and then sort out its internal contradictions (represented here as black and white), this is a special creative act! In the biblical Book of Genesis (as well as in the myths of many other cultures), the creation story narrates how day and night, the separation of light and darkness, were made on the first day of creation. Possibly, the card shows a situation of a personal creation, of an awakening from ignorance or ambiguity. This is a reason for great joy.

Get accustomed to it, but without pressure. Relax. Your freedom is not a burden. You are perfect the way you are. Be prepared to be completely here and now, to act upon your own yearnings and to respond to what is happening all around you. It is your responsibility. You do not need to prove anything. Befriend and love yourself.

The other side: Something dawns on you. You are scared. Darkness is falling. This can't go on. You need to get up and escape so that your present situation will not turn into a prison or a grave. You have been chasing false ideas for far too long. This development can still be reversed. You chose in your past, but you can choose differently now and in your future. Get up!

Be aware of and protect yourself against rash responses. Put two ≺ *Advice*
and two together! Get acquainted presently to new knowledge
and concepts.

1 – 10 June

A time of being conscious

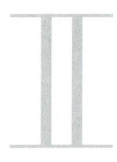

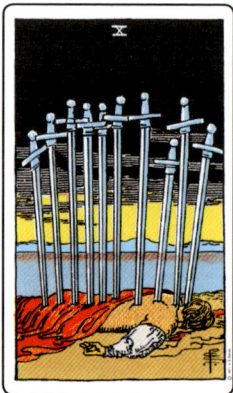

Ten Swords

3rd decan of Gemini (11 – 21 June)

To symbolize a cornucopia of spirit this card doesn't show a guru or philosopher king but rather—and to the contrary—the end of all role models. Your former self-definition lies stretched out on the ground, it is your ego, the image you have created of yourself. Perhaps a certain concept of love, happiness or success has died. This may be painful, shattering, or liberating. What matters is that you are still alive! You are the butterfly, and here, in front of you, lies the chrysalis you've hatched from.

Start to take possession of your life and your freedom. There are so many "right" ways and solutions. Let unproductive dreams, concepts and theories die in order to have a new and shining horizon appear. Replace lifeless concepts, constant control and useless justifications by your ability to accept the present moment and to make decisions in the present situation—by becoming transparent and open, alert for what the moment requires.

Our thoughts and decisions commit us: unfit and unproductive thoughts can ruin us. In the best case, however, the seed will bear ripe fruit, and out of our personal existence, out of devotion to pure existence, a consciousness grows which bestows great happiness and deep satisfaction: consciousness as being conscious, that is, spiritual consciousness in and resulting from a conscious life.

Advice ➤ **Be ready to act, even without role models. Let your breath and your thought be a quiet river. Stop thinking about everything.**

Back to the Roots

The Cancer Month (22 June – 22 July)

The beginning of summer leads us to the deepest point in the astrological yearly cycle. This sign of the zodiac is defined by "I feel", its element is Water. The animal cancer, or crab, represents an early stage of our evolution. So, the beginning of summer leads us back to our origins: whether that is the family, our mother especially, or prenatal experiences.

We come into contact with our sources. Sometimes we find we need to clean them. This is the time of year for many ancient customs which center on springs, water, and baptism (for example, June 24 is the feast day of John the Baptist). In earlier times, Christian baptism was celebrated by completely submerging an adult in a river or a basin. The old ego had to drown and dissolve to be reborn as a new "I". Fairy tales speak of this very experience when they tell the story of the fountain of youth. It is the secret of the "complete inner renewal" which we can always experience at this time of year.

*Conscious will
and karma*

THE CHARIOT

THE HIGH PRIESTESS

*Soul, your own spirit;
own opinions*

*A rich life of the soul and
an open ear*

QUEEN of CUPS

VII-The Chariot

How we drive through life: The upper part represents our conscious will, while the lower part depicted by the stone, is the unconscious substructure, the karma, the history of our life. In this we are grounded and struck, we can't just get out of it, but we can always give our chariot a new direction.

II-The High Priestess

Sovereignty and fertility of the soul. Chances and dangers of individuality. The book of personal significances, your personal script, your own opinion.

Queen of Cups

Wealth, beauty, and sovereignty of the inner life. To achieve this mastery, we need to take possession of our own emotions (this is why the lid of the cup is closed); at the same time, we need to have a friendly, open ear for others (see the shell-shaped throne).

22 June – 22 July

A time of returning joy

1ˢᵗ decan of Cancer
(22 June –1 July)

Two Cups

Each year, this decan leads us back to our "sources". The joy we have been experiencing and will come to experience is one of the best reasons, the best driving force for a satisfying and fulfilling "long journey through a brief life." You can always return to those joys you've experienced, to those moments of bliss, and they will always fill you with new strength.

At first glance, this is an image of love and friendship. But we need to look closer. What do the cups contain? Have we not all had to empty a bitter cup once or twice? Each year we need to choose afresh here. Especially with emotional and intimate questions, everybody has the right to choose and decide for themselves. Tell the others what you expect from them and what you are willing to give. End what does not make fun anymore. Get rid of all which sours your joy.

Often we look for our "better half" in a partner, and still we are deeply disappointed. And then we discover these missing pieces in ourselves—and become open for the other for his or her self's sake, not as a part or continuation of our own needs! Care about the hopes and fears. Learn to differentiate, especially concerning emotions. The clearer the differences between partners, the more fruitful is what they have in common.

Clarify hopes and fears. Deal with other people. Let it flow! Get ≺ *Advice into the flow. Indulge and be enchanted!*

22 June – 1 July

A time of flowing feelings

Three Cups

*2ⁿᵈ decan of Cancer
(2 – 12 July)*

Another source of joy in life: happiness to be ready for yourself and others. A group or constellation to which you completely belong, where you have totally arrived, into which you give yourself completely, not to waste or sacrifice yourself, but from the pure joy of being, from the joy of giving. These are those moments in your life where you smile in harmony with the world, in which a moment is eternity, a time of pure bliss in which everything is possible.

This is one of the most beautiful cards of the whole Tarot deck if we regard it as an image of overflowing, prosperous emotions, as an image of a ripe human and inner life. And yet the card warns against emotional and internal dependency. The way the women hold the cups represents not only the beauty, but also the arrogance of souls. Success is also a thing of your emotions. The right word at the right place can do wonders and set the world in motion. Don't allow others to decide on the value of your emotions. Accept other's feelings even if you can't identify with them.

Advice ➢ *Don't be afraid of "emotional" reactions. But understand what you feel. Be open to others or withdraw, even if it feels a bit funny at first. Your soul will be able to bear several truths at the same time. Let your soul grow. This is a good time for old and new friendships.*

A time of soul renewal

3rd decan of Cancer
(13 – 22 July)

Four Cups

Find time for yourself! Relax and have a good time. Meditate or finish what hinders you to meditate. In rest you will find words and phrases for experiences and tasks where so far there was only speechlessness.

What were your original goals? You now need to process, perhaps even newly evaluate, your inner experiences and expectations. Contemplate to deal with the past and be open for everything new. Some things have been neglected and need to be done now. Although this card can mean, at times, that you should withdraw yourself, that you should get a good sleep and dream, the general signs do not suggest withdrawal, but growth.

Do not become melancholic. Melancholia is an inverted stubbornness. It numbs the senses. In contrast: you should do everything to awaken your senses, to quiet them and give them wings. Unusual opportunities offer themselves, and these are the order of the day! Encountering nature (either the nature outside or your inner nature: all that which is—and should be—natural for you) will give you inner peace. Learn and enjoy to stay within yourself and to listen to your inner stream.

The fourth cup symbolizes (the soul's) productivity and creativity. It represents new insights and invitations—which you may accept or reject.

*Let your soul grow wings. Don't expect anything special. Open up ◅ **Advice** for inspiration. This is the best thing to do at the moment.*

Just be human—be a human whole

The Leo Month (23 July – 22 August)

The days are long, light and warmth are here in abundance (if it doesn't rain too much …). It is the holiday season, a time of ripening (Lughnasadh), and of light and shadow.—The sun, powerful as it is, casts sharp shadows and shines its light into ditches and deep pits. Especially because summer awakens lust for life and a certain lightness in us, those regions we generally tend to ignore make themselves felt.

"I want" defines this sign of the zodiac, Fire is its element. So many adventures we have to undergo (and no-one is fitter for them than the lion in us) until we finally loose the shadows of our past which were still clinging to us—often without us recognizing them. We need much experience and success until we have brought our most important future hopes and promises into our life here and now. To live in full force means to be completely present in the here and now. And this is the point: be present as a whole person, gather all forces in the focus of the very moment.

Urges and being wild,
wisdom and thinking

STRENGTH

THE SUN

Power of life and joy,
being conscious

Acid test and
true will

KING of WANDS

VIII-Strength

The red lion and the white woman represent the most powerful aspects of human nature: wild and wise. "As above—so below": People have two lust centers—one between the legs, and the other between their ears! Yet both persons on the image also warn against all our unconscious drives, those that, since Carl Jung, have been called Anima and Animus: animal urges and wild, idealistic thinking.

XIX-The Sun

Life force and joy. Being aware and conscious. Especially the second birth (when, as an adult, you re-birth yourself and choose your relatives and where your home is).

King of Wands

Just like a salamander this person can walk right through fire without dying. Yes, as "King of Wands" you always need new acid tests to force your will into the open. So go ahead with all your might to reach the hopes of your heart.

23 July – 22 August

A time of playful success

Five Wands

1st *decan of Leo*
(23 July – 2 August)

Take part! Play, confrontation, competition of different energies, half-grown and freshly grown interest and intentions, even within you. Only if you keep "many fires" burning, your personal will is recreated and remains alive.

This also concerns a new culture of play which is more than just children's games or entertainment. This is nothing bad, but to *regard the whole life as a play, without gamboling*, is what this is all about. You start by creating space for many inclinations and interests. Fire does go out if it does not move, will without opportunity wears itself out.

Your will goes out and is recreated every moment, the picture shows that as a still. We see young people here, this means that especially the growing shoots within you contribute to the confrontation at hand and in the new formulation of your will.

You open up for the play of forces—within you, with you, and all around you. You will be touched by people, ideas, and events in your surroundings. Play with them and feel the energy. You may use external, even "enemy" energies for your own goals in a kind of creative Aikido or exchange of blows.

Advice ➤ **Don't be frightened and don't run away. Decide the goals you aim to achieve: do really make up your mind, and then go on. Doing things by halves will destroy you in the end.**

A time of gathering forces

2ⁿᵈ decan of Leo
(3 – 12 August)

Six Wands

This section of the year encourages us to assemble all our strengths and weaknesses and to reach out for a new success with all our effort!

We display optimal force whenever we use our strengths and weaknesses in common. Act, don't hide your light under a bushel. Yet do not hide your "small" or weak aspects. Quite the contrary—if you follow those things you feel a weakness for, they will strengthen you! If you consider your strengths and weaknesses, you will be secure in your efforts, you remain flexible, and you will be able to respond in a "holistic" way.

This is urgent too, as something is in movement here, something that is still "green", that means young and inexperienced! The questions you have will only receive complex answers, neither simple nor one-dimensional. Complex answers actually enlarge your leeway and the range of your possibilities.

Stand for what motivates you internally, stand for it with all your effort. Don't play a hero who doesn't know weaknesses, but also refrain from a false shyness and powerless humility which does not expect anything from your own strengths. Follow what you feel a weakness for, and advocate your inner convictions. You will be like a runaway fire. Nothing will be able to stop you!

Show your strengths and weaknesses, even in love and sexuality. ≺ Advice
Don't let yourself be intimidated, also, do not pressure others!

A time of courage

Seven Wands

3rd decan of Leo
(13 – 22 August)

You are "top"! Blind actions and ambition now can only do harm. A new level will be decisive, an alert style when you use your own strength. This is what summer teaches us: overcome faint-heartedness and blind zealousness; do not look for happiness in dramatic scenes or reactions of defiance. Try to react to special challenges with awareness and a heightened presence, not with stress or tension. Breathe, show your abilities, and keep track of everything!

In this way, you learn to achieve more while, at the same time, you don't wear yourself. It is a wonder, and it is wonderful! And yet it is nothing mysterious, but can easily be explained: as we master tasks, languages, or daily routine as a matter of course in a way we could never have imagined as a child, we are able to reach a fitting and personal sovereignty in dealing with complex energies and many tasks at the same time.

We can learn from children how to deal playfully with a new situation. Just as children play, completely focused on what they are doing, moving on, and starting anew, always 100 percent present, with fascination, not pressure.

Advice ➤ **Don't let yourself be provoked, and don't provoke others! Find a place which stresses your sovereignty and keeps, even increases, your power in the long run!**

Ripening and Harvest

The Virgo Month
(23 August – 21 September)

The perfection of summer, time of harvest feasts in many traditions and old tales. But also the motif of harvest in life: What has ripened? What can be harvested at this very moment? What needs cultivation, which field requires a new seeding?

"I analyze" defines this sign. Its element is Earth. This part of the yearly cycle recalls pleasure and ripening. "Whoever believes that all fruits are ripe when strawberries are ripe does know nothing about grapes." *(Paracelsus).* Grapes demand hard work in the vineyard, and yet they also signify sweet pleasure—the pleasure of our senses, of sensuality ("celebrate feasts" like the god of wine, Dionysos, lat. Bacchus), as well as our pleasure derived from sense and meaning ("in vino veritas"—"in wine there is truth").

Asceticism and withdrawal, the presence of God

THE HERMIT

THE MAGICIAN

Uniqueness and fresh solutions

Light and darkness, talents and handicaps

KNIGHT of PENTACLES

IX-The Hermit

Stressing the asceticism and withdrawal of the card misses its deeper meaning. The historical hermits were searching for a place where they could live "in the presence of God." In all religions, this is regarded as the highest goal, the greatest bliss, that man can ever reach. Ripening and harvest will be a success if we find the way to and with "God."

I-The Magician

On our own, holistic path of life we can find solutions which by far transcend any model. This is distinctively magic, but not of the supernatural kind. It presents itself as opportunity. Nobody can show you how to do it, and nobody can take it away from you.

Knight of Pentacles

Few cards in the Waite-Tarot have so much contrast as this, with its strong yellow and black. We need to understand and accept our bright and shadowy sides, talents and handicaps, and to bring them to fruition on the fields of life! Even the crap we produce from time to time will be useful as manure. Forgive yourself and others for not being perfect.

23 August – 21 September

A time of mastering

1st decan of Virgo
(23 August – 2 September)

E ach task you finish reflects the work you do with yourself. The more you sharpen your talents and accept your limitations, the more you will be master or mistress of your own good. You master the *multiplication* of your own talents. Create many events that bear your handwriting, that are of your own making, and in which you can recognize yourself.

Eight Pentacles

"Summer will come full circle." This section of the yearly cycle reminds us to enjoy what we are doing. Remember that it is not only the results that count, but also all that happens along the way. In your life, you are the boss. Proceed step by step. Then your work resembles a growing organism, and you may grow with it. This makes your work positive, and creates rich results which are well worth the effort. A situation of personal affluence, not the luxury of bragging and wasting, but the affluence of well-being, realized ideas, and wishes fulfilled, "much was unnecessary/and yet, just that/should have been the most important" *(Edith Vahrenhorst).* You have mastered the art of the necessary. Awareness is what counts. Not everything works in an instant, you need patience for much of what you do. But this will not harm you.

Relax, but stay alert. Learn to read "between the lines". Be pre- ◁ *Advice*
pared to learn something new. Be careful not to teach others
arrogantly.

A time of harvest

Nine Pentacles

2nd decan of Virgo (3 – 12 September)

2nd decan of Virgo (3 – 12 September)

There is a lot of difference whether you are in this world or not. You bring something that enriches the Earth. Therefore, don't hide your talents! Be generous and show your fellow humans what treasures you have to offer, because you yourself are a *treasure*.

What does the hedge mean? Does it protect or obstruct? How do you live? The grapes are a sign of harvest and of indulgence, but they are also a symbol of hard work in the vineyard. The small snail in the foreground warns us not to be sluggish or overtly thin-skinned. On the other side, it symbolizes that we should carry our house with us and be at home at any place. The falcon symbolizes the art to grip things, yet warns against a headless hunt for happiness!

If you treat yourself and your fellow humans with respect and love, you will have a prosperous and comfortable situation in your life in which everybody has his or her own realm—and in which you, with your strengths and weaknesses, with your advantages and disadvantages, in short, with all you are, will find a home. There is no greater gain than this—and you should not be satisfied with less!

Advice ➤ *Stop hunting through life like a falcon and then return into your shell. "Only if it is cut will a rose bloom": relinquish unnecessary ideals, unwanted commitments and vague experiments. Develop your own meaningful rules and live accordingly!*

A time of rich results

3rd decan of Virgo
(13 – 22 September)

Ten Pentacles

Everything is here. You just need to let it into your life. The greatest wealth is to recognize your own contribution to what is happening in the world.

Your own experiences and those of others all come together to form a larger whole. Regard yourself as part of creation, of the cosmic flow. You know that what you do is based on what the ancients did before you, and the young ones will continue with it. Time is only relative. You find yourself in the old and in the new. Nothing ever gets lost. Nothing keeps you away from living, from feeling your blood pulse, from staying or going.

Love is not only the measure for intimate relationships. Love is a dependable orientation in the web of daily encounters and events. Risk some more love and less exclusivity with it. Care lovingly for many people and many events in your life.

You will find happiness, satisfying relationships, and a home. All you need is already here. The well-being of your soul as well as your material well-being. A balance in movement. A fullness of possibilities and inspiration. A frame of reference which clearly marks your surroundings, yet also reflects the whole universe. The experience of firm roots and arrival: you can let yourself "fall" where you are at home, and where you let yourself "fall," you create yourself a home.

Promote talents in as many people as possible. Face those tasks others ask you for – this will bring you great success. ≺ *Advice*

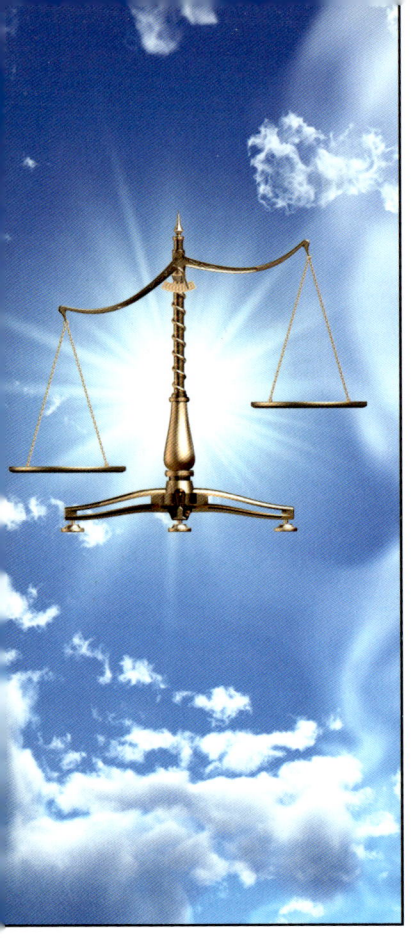

What has weight in life?

The Libra Month
(23 September – 22 October)

Autumnal equinox, day and night are of equal length. A symbol of balance, also in the scales of Libra. Although by now nights are becoming longer than days, and nature outside and the vegetation withdraw and begin to prepare for rest, human experience must become awake rather than withdraw now. The yearly astrological cycle has reached its turning point, for the first time it now enters the upper half, the so-called day-half, of the zodiac.

Aries is the first sign of the complete yearly cycle, the proverbial pioneer (transforming desert into a garden); but Libra is a pioneer in the mental and conscious realms of mankind. This zodiacal sign is defined as "I adjust". Air is its element. We are talking about the development of our consciousness which will enable us to balance mistakes and deficiencies, and to deal wisely and justly with wishes and fears, talents and handicaps.

XI-Justice

All this is expressed by this Great Card. Through the weapons of the intellect (libra and sword) desires, urges, and affects (represented by

Truth, honesty and being conscious

JUSTICE

THE EMPRESS

Woman and mother, naturalness

Injuries and rigidity or freedom and ease

QUEEN of SWORDS

the dominant red in the robe of Justice) will be measured, judged, and balanced. The conscious handling of emotions, preferences, and dislikes gives us joy and freedom.

III-The Empress

This card also expresses conscious wishes. Ostensibly about the experience as a woman or mother, its backbone is the important question: who runs your life, who rules what is natural for you. How can you express—and enjoy—what is natural and self-evident for you?

Queen of Swords

We decide on how we use the weapons of our intellect (the powers of our mind). The sword can also harm, it petrifies us or others (like the petrified butterfly and the stone child's head at the throne); or we solve our troubles and fears, our hopes and wishes and become light and free like the butterflies that crown the Queen's head.

23 September – 22 October

A time of reflection

Two Swords

1st decan of Libra
(23 September – 2 October)

You reached for the swords, the weapons of your mind. The ocean of emotions and instincts is close and familiar. You remain at the place where day merges into dream, where sleep meets being awake. Keep this door open. There is no point in locking yourself in or in blocking your access to emotions. Learn to differentiate between emotion and simple fantasy, and you will gain insight into realms way beyond pure outer appearance. Just as the radio operator contacts distant continents, you will gain insight and understanding of realms of life and soul that are way beyond anything that you have ever experienced.

Outer appearance doesn't help. It is better to interpret emotions and dreams, to "digest" experiences. Ambivalence, ambiguity, and inconsistency are a part of life. Even the cornucopia of so many conflicting experiences will not discourage you and you do not search for safety in indecisiveness or coquetry. The better you learn to differentiate between fantasy and reality, the easier you come to rest. New friends, a new lightness of being, especially in your partnership, will reward you.

Advice ➤ **Involve your imagination, and success will follow. There is no absolute wrong or right but you will find what is right for you now. Do what needs to be done: "Qui vivra verra" ("Those who live will see.")**

23 September – 2 October

A time of realization

2nd decan of Libra
(3 – 12 October)

Three Swords

T hree swords pierce the heart and may mean pain and harm which you either suffer or do unto others. On the other side, think of the image of Amor's arrow going straight into a heart. It's a popular motif: There are ways of touching a heart that are beneficial!

Mind (swords) and emotions (heart), heart and intellect meet and dovetail. Conscious thoughts penetrate to those issues that the heart feels inside. What the heart at first knows only fleetingly and in its initial stage will be made known and become conscious through the swords. You realize what is in your heart and what you can do for it!

If you draw this card you should stop fooling yourself or others. Risk being more sincere. You will only gain. Don't hide what goes on inside your heart. Breathe into your suffering until you can let go. There is a solution, and you will find it now.

The power of honesty. Don't let problems paralyze you, and don't let them anger you. Inevitably, there will be burdens we have to carry as well as evitable worries which we can master. The great, fruitful and comforting force of our mind lies in its ability to balance deficiencies and mistakes. Use it!

Get to the point, stick to the essential. Discover what moves your ◄ *Advice*
heart, begin to do what you really want to do. This card represents quietness, concentration, inner meditation, and ripening. Maybe you have done so much and experienced so much that it now needs an outlet, or important events loom up on the horizon.

3 – 12 October

A time of mental work

Four Swords

3rd decan of Libra
(13 – 22 October)

This is an image of great mental concentration and of a pure conscience, or, on the other side, of mental inflexibility, paralyzing thoughts, and stupefaction. There may be experiences that put us out of action for a while. But at the same time the card speaks about beautiful experiences of deep inner peace.

Be that as it may, we are here not dealing with exterior, but mental concepts. The left figure in the window carries the letters PAX in her halo. This means peace. It is about personal contentment and inner peace.

So many impressions have to be processed, until many tiny stones form one mosaic, until the jigsaw puzzle is completed. To form one single coherent image from so many thoughts and experiences is the positive aspect of the gift of imagination—and this is what you need right now. Yet the issue is meditation as well, the collection and the flow of the mind. Like the artist or athlete who—although he has so often done a certain performance before—still needs to freshly concentrate and prepare himself.

Don't be a victim of dead ideals. With a good conscience you feel light and lively. Your self-imposed distance to the hectic hustle and bustle enables your inner wisdom to come to light.

Advice ➤ *The more you use your mental capacities to the full, the stronger they get. Only the mind that is never used wears quickly. Whether your ideas are wrong or right shows when you keep a calm head even in moments of great pressure.*

13 – 22 October

True Longing

The Scorpio Month
(23 October – 21 November)

The middle of autumn is an eerie time for many: It is the time of Halloween and Samhain, of commemorating the dead, but also the feast day of Reformation (31 October) and—in many regions—the beginning of Shrovetide (11 November).

These issues are only apparently disfigured. The Scorpio Month is all about the spiritual home in the world. Man differs from all other animals in having a spirit; only he knows that he will eventually die. This frightens, estranges, and finds its expression in the feast days of the dead. Remembering our forefathers has its comforts, too: they back us, they give us power and advice. And future generations will be able to build on our lives.

Keeping in mind that dying is an integral part of life helps to find out what one wants from life—and what not. This is why the astrological definition of Scorpio says: "I desire" (element: Water).

It is also not by chance that the season of Shrovetide begins at this time of year: our awareness that we live a unique life enables us to enjoy life, even if it is 11/11 (practically "5 to 12"). There is a fitting sentence from Martin Luther, who was born in the sign of Scorpio (on November 10):

23 October – 21 November

Something ends, letting
lose and a new life

Fulfillment of wishes,
reduction of anxiety

DEATH

JUDGMENT

Change and renewal,
our true destiny

KING of CUPS

"Even if I knew that tomorrow the world would go to pieces, I would still plant my apple tree."

XIII-Death
This is not the last of the Great Cards of the Tarot, but number XIII. Death is a part of life. It is not its end …

XX-Judgement
… here we need to overcome all egoism, and spiritual zeal as well, to find out what our true destination is.

King of Cups
Fulfilling wishes and reducing fears results in the desirable state in which we are perfectly happy without any wishes left.

23 October – 21 November

A time of change

Five Cups

1st decan of Scorpio
(23 October – 1 November)

You encounter great emotions you've never known before. Don't be superstitious: The black figure does indeed recall darkness and blackness. But also have in mind the figure of a chimney sweeper: The unknown can also be a source of joy, as it offers new and positive possibilities.

Offer yourself and others nothing but the plain truth. It is better to accept a truth rather too late than never. A disillusion also involves the taking away of an illusion, it is a means of letting go illusion and entering into a new clarity.

The soul acts as a mirror. The psyche especially sees those things as dark for which no image yet exists which it could reflect. Of all that is really new for it, the soul has only the darkest hints! Such hints, dark dreams and similar things may be a first warning signal of an unusual danger. Call for help immediately in such a case. A black-out of the soul may—to see it positively—also indicate that something completely new begins: a metamorphosis, a phase of changing, and a dark section of your life—the beginning of a new stage in life. The end of a leg of a distance in which you've learned your lesson may release enormous energies.

Don't run away from your emotions! Take time and space for an inner renaissance. Admit tears as well as fresh enthusiasm. Get help, if necessary. And be prepared to give help and support. Let it flow. ◅ *Advice*

A time of remembrance

Six Cups

2nd *decan of Scorpio (2 – 11 November)*

Old dreams and deep seated desires surface and show—like the image—two faces. (Don't be surprised if at first glance you can only discern one—this is normal.) Note the double posture of the little woman: She looks away from the manikin, yet she also looks at the manikin. Which of these postures do you discern easily, and which not?

Our memories of our childhood (of the soul) show that same double face of joy and sadness, of experienced acceptance and rejection.

Open up for memories, dreams, and intuition, even when they seem to concern trivia. Look carefully into your emotional experience. What was good then, what was bad? How can what was beautiful then happen again, how can I prevent the bad things from happening again? Today, you have far more alternatives dealing with wishes and fears. Discern your feelings.

The right occasion to investigate your memories, to dig up old photos and notes. Look after (your) children. Support the inner child within you! Let go childish ways to react and do what you wanted to do for a long time as an adult! Take your chance to get rid of old fears and fulfill your heart's desire!

Advice ➤ *Success will be a result of your openness for happy surprises, for small and big wonders. We need to discover them again in everyday life: "unless you become like little children ..."*

A time for wishing

Seven Cups

Undreamt of, fantastic worlds reveal themselves to you. Choose what you wish and take it! But remember: you may experience yourself with your head in the clouds, a victim of unsteady illusions.

The Seven Cups represent gifts and presents of a promising, yet deterring meaning. The head symbolizes beauty, but also vanity. The towering castle means power and might, on the other side, distance and loneliness. Pearls and jewels speak for themselves. The cup on the side carries a laurel wreath: a wreath for the dead or the wreath of victory, success or futility. The dragon symbolizes the forces of the underworld with their devouring or luck bringing meaning. The serpent signifies wisdom, but also falsehood and low motives. Finally, the seventh cup is empty; it represents new possibilities but also missed opportunities.

You have little choice but to test your current needs and personal goals. Sometimes, it is just that greatest desire and that "unrealistic" longing which is perfect for you. And there are cases in which even the tiniest temptation and most harmless promise are of evil.

Find out what is behind your fears and follow those wishes which ◄ *Advice*
radiate the greatest energy. "By their fruits you will know" what is
right for you and what is not. Find and uphold your own measure,
especially concerning love and intimate wishes.

Arts and tasks of living

The Sagittarius Month (22 November – 21 December)

Three things intermingle in the month of Sagittarius: the end of the calendar year, the preparation of Christmas (Advent season), and the continuation of the questions asked by Scorpio (What do you really want? What do you need to be perfectly happy?). The list of wishes we traditionally note down in the time before Christmas encompasses all these attempts and tasks. At the same time, the list of wishes and the Advent calendar are symbols; they represent the destinations and the legs of our journey through life. The sign of Sagittarius inquires about our plans and our tasks in life. It deals with goals and long-term visions. Its definition: "I see." Fire is its element.

XIV-Temperance

In the ancient world, "temperance" was regarded as one of the four cardinal virtues. This concerned—and still concerns—the keeping of measure. About finding harmonious solutions for great opposites which are literally dissolved, bridged, and

The measure of things, solutions for opposites

TEMPERANCE

WHEEL of FORTUNE

Destiny, luck, and opportunities

Great energies, but also lean spells

KNIGHT of WANDS

then integrated. We are not talking about mediocrity or banalities. The Great Works of Life *(opus magnum)* are life-tasks, they require a life-long effort with many changes and by-ways. Look at the long path in the image: it is about goals which will bring out the "angel" in you, your higher self, your greatest possibilities, and will bring them to bear!

X-The Wheel of Fortune

The open books signify wisdom and education, the understanding of connections and interrelations. Thus, it becomes easy for us to find our luck and our opportunities in our destiny.

Knight of Wands

"What do I want to achieve, how far will I go? What plans do I have for my luck?" The image warns against losing the way and becoming struck, and encourages mastering lean spells and focusing on the great aims of life. This culmination is also represented by the pyramids shown in the image.

22 November – 21 December

A time of enthusiasm

Eight Wands

1st decan of Sagittarius
(22 November – 1 December)

This card signifies "successful transfer of energies," the ability to move others and let yourself be moved. Your efforts show results, and these confront you with new challenges. You possess so many talents, and much has now to be brought to a new result. This is a demanding situation which threatens that you lose yourself completely.

Prepare yourself for this giant step. Only you can realize your dreams. "Take your broken wings and learn to fly. All your life, you were only waiting for this moment to arise. Blackbird fly," as the Beatles so beautifully express it in their song "Blackbird." Have the courage to reach new experiences and impressions.

And yet this is also the card of projections and of jugglery. Projections are a blown-up version of wishful thinking. One's inner urges and desires are projected outward—one encounters one's own emotions and needs as seemingly coming from outside, as ghosts or seemingly objective facts. This does not happen in the head, or in the stomach, or in emotions, it resembles a film in which you are an unknowing actor. Self-control and control from the outside is what you need now.

Advice ➢ **Stop this unwanted state of indecision. You cannot put your dreams into action in a dream. Show up and realize the magic that hides within you! You will find help and support from many.**

A time of exploration

2nd decan of Sagittarius
(2 – 11 December)

Nine Wands

The bind on the head of the image's figure is possibly a bandage and signals a wounded, single-minded consciousness; or this bind is the badge of a warrior on his path and signifies an *alertness of the whole surroundings.*

If the head is bandaged, this also points at bound thoughts and insights. The left and right hemisphere of the brain is going to be connected to *one another.* "Our heads are round so our thoughts can change direction." *(Francis Picabia).* Not only our thinking, but also our ability to observe and understand.

What is happening? What is developing? To ponder these questions protects you from unwise and hasty decisions and actions. The attentive consideration and examination of all urges and motives requires and develops a holistic and protective intuition.

Intuition causes a finer perception of all that happens in front and in the back of the eye. Sharpen your ears, focus your vision, but at the same time relax in order to be able to perceive *all.* Ignore rumors, be skeptical of pure assumptions and simple claims. The solution that you need at the moment is to live your life more fully, to get more from life.

Reduce unfounded fears, fulfill important wishes! Still focusing ≺ *Advice* *attention on all effective developments and changes, understand that there is a task which at this time demands all your attention.*

A time of arrival

Ten Wands

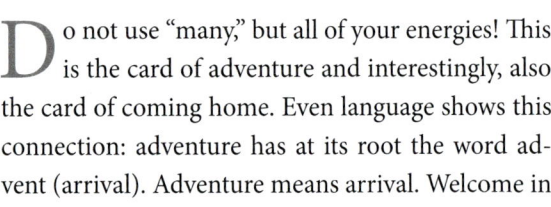

3rd decan of Sagittarius (12 – 21 December)

Do not use "many," but all of your energies! This is the card of adventure and interestingly, also the card of coming home. Even language shows this connection: adventure has at its root the word advent (arrival). Adventure means arrival. Welcome in life!

The focus here is completely in the advanced and proposed energies, projects, interests, and intentions. You see metaphorically what it means to follow your *inclination*. You have to incline, to enter completely. Just as you progress quicker on a steep mountain path if you walk slightly inclined, the human figure on this image carries home the fruits of his efforts far more easily by leaning towards the Wands. They are, so to speak, close to the heart.

Only when you unhesitatingly love people, events, or topics, will you be able to understand them in their own logic. You need lean forward, advance with courage and completely enter. In this way, you will be ahead of the rest. But if you feel that you have burdened yourself too much, throw off ballast and understand from scratch what it is all about!

Advice ➢ *Use all your energy. Let a hundred flowers bloom. Be careful not to waste your energies! Don't give up effort until you have actually exhausted all your possibilities.*

On our Peak

The Capricorn Month (22 December – 19 January)

The beginning of winter leads us to the summit on the yearly cycle. Capricorns live high up on the mountains, and the sign leads us to our *highest performances*. And just like not all peaks are of equal height, there are also different high performances. Each person reaches his or her highest peak at the point where they have most fully realized their possibilities. In these peak experiences we get a glimpse of sense and meaning in a very special way.

XV-The Devil

It appears paradoxical that this should be the typical Great Card of the time of Capricorn, as this also includes Christmas and the New Year. And yet it is a fitting card: the time is all about bringing light into darkness. We have to accept our "horns," the animalistic and wild aspects of our personality. Seen by the light of day, it is not difficult to differentiate between them: on the one hand, the "devil" is a kind of vampire, something still not civilized (in us), which molests us and exhausts us, and we are rightfully afraid of it. Yet this is a "devil" we can get rid of

Darkness, dependency, or light and liberation

THE DEVIL

XXI

THE WORLD

Completion and realization

Talents and success, realism and care

QUEEN of PENTACLES

as soon as we recognize it.—On the other hand, the "devil" represents a deprived child, something at our very roots (in us) which we have neglected despite our longing for it. We can now bring it home.—As long as these two sides of the "devil" have not yet been separated, this image conveys very mixed feelings …

XXI-The World

… and yet the images shows, once more, your own differentiation and connecting of these (and further) contradictions in life. Going by numbers, it is the highest of the cards.

Queen of Pentacles

"I use," is the definition of Capricorn. Its element is Earth. We here see the fitting "Queen" of tolls and talents. Her abilities as a sovereign person with so many talents, a sense of realism, and care, are much needed. Expect a rose garden in the blue mountains!

A Time of Reassessment

1st decan of Capricorn
(22 – 31 December)

The two faces of the same coin: your sunny and your dark sides. How were you coined, what would you like to imprint? You now need to see the "pentacles" (tolls and talents) in a new combination (cf. the green ribbon in the image).

There will be a change in what you consider to be of worth. You can—and you need—to clarify what is fact. Take stock and draw a balance—also person-ally. Make use of this time at the end of the year. Pay

Two Pentacles

attention to the "coincidences" which occur in your life. Your chances and tasks are connected to the way you manage to wriggle out of prac-tical constraints which are nothing but assumptions. There simply is an alternative—always at least one! We are talking about your aptness and experience in handling your challenges.

A reassessment of experiences and tasks often is preceded by new points of view and new ideas (cf. the cocked head of the figure in the image). When the reality you're used to changes, you have to count with unexpected confirmation but also with uncertainty. This will hap-pen in a holistic and practical way, you will even feel it in your body. Sometimes in these periods of change (and no matter how old we are), in these phases of a real change of personal ways, our senses appear to be turned upside down. Don't allow yourself to be wound up! If you want to spread the wings of your personality, it is a blessing already.

"Invest" in the development of your personality. It will do you ≺ Advice some good and promotes your talents at the same time.

A Time of Processing the Unknown

Three Pentacles

2nd decan of Capricorn (1 – 10 January)

This image shows a stonemason who—slightly raised on a bench—is working with his mallet. Monk and fool, or monk and nun, represent the ordering party or colleagues, audience and consumer of this work.

Different aspects of work, profession, and calling are the topics here: working with materials, redefining the surroundings, working with yourself, releasing inner powers and forces. But also the work with and beside others. And questions: What does this work contribute to? To whom will it be of use? For what will it provide the fundamentals?

Don't let yourself be betrayed and do not shy away from controversial dark or unknown things. You will discover hidden talents! If you want to reach new heights, be prepared to also descend into the depths. Your light will be most needed where darkness is the blackest. It will actually be of most use there!

You do not consider work as a necessary evil only. To you, it also means fulfillment and pleasure—and a calling as well: "If you love what you do, you never need work again" *(Confucius)*.

Advice ➤ *Follow your calling and you will find work that is meaningful for you. Your commitment will lead to a new way of work. There is a certain point where it is not results or deadlines that really count, but your complete work process. You will learn that what you do is part of a greater whole, and that is it effective; that even seemingly unimportant or minor actions constitute an important part of what you do.*

1 – 10 January

A Time of Appreciation

3rd decan of Capricorn (11 – 19 January)

B e a master practitioner in your own right: keep what is important and dear for you. Discover the world and make yourself at home in it.

Each and everybody have special talents and special handicaps. Don't assume the role of either the hero or the loser. Your strengths and your weaknesses have their own worth. Make sure they pay off. The most important talents are those which create the most benefit. They are of most use when they fulfill the most wishes and reduce the most fears.

Four Pentacles

Love is not only a question of emotions. Love also means a mutual support in creating an existence. Hand the key to your heart over to others. Stress the specialness of your situation. Let others share your world.

Your very own special character is defined by what you are able to do and what you possess. With your skills and abilities you create satisfying possessions, a solid basis. Enjoy your qualities, and stand by what you can. Don't pay attention to boastful people or simple yes-men.

Sometimes this card means that it is important to set limits more ≺ *Advice*
consciously, to stress what you are worth or even to discover what you are worth. Sometimes it asks you to communicate more fully, to let as many others as possible share in your own skills and abilities. Have regard for the community, for society. But you can also expect the other's regard for your special talents and tasks.

Freedom and wholeness

The Aquarius Month (20 January – 18 February)

It is the middle of winter but the days are growing longer again. This is why festivals of the returning light are being celebrated: Imbolc or St. Brigid's Day (in the Germanic and Celtic tradition on February 1), and, with a similar meaning, Candlemas (in the Christian tradition on February 2). These festival days are also important dates to seize the opportunity for fresh perspectives and visions of the new year.

Aquarius is ruled by Uranus. This correlates especially with "The Fool." All that is archaic and primordial is connected to this mythological figure, as well as the modern tradition of enlightenment, of anarchy, of opposition to the ruling classes. In brief, the topics of Aquarius are a free spirit, brilliance, an all-encompassing knowledge, but at the same time also getting lost in yourself, narcissism, as well as ruthlessness.

XVII-The Star

It is the time to reflect on your own position within the universe. It is us that perceive and create "all." We need to understand our own part in the creation. This is exactly what the jars of the star woman express:

Our part in creation

THE STAR

THE FOOL

Beginning and ending, freedom

Connect heart and brain in wisdom

KING of SWORDS

she *draws* water (in a way, creating it to filter it, to sort it, to make it productive). We are talking about the "naked truth" here, about honesty and originality. But the card also shows the figure of Narcissus who is in love with himself.

0/22-The Fool

All or nothing—zero as a symbol encompasses both: it warns against an empty, unfulfilled life; and it encourages completing the great circle of life, to experience all of life's colors and to focus them—until they again become white.

King of Swords

Aquarius is defined by "I know." Its element is the Air. Fittingly, we here see the master of the weapons of the mind. If he understands the symbols visible on his throne (butterflies, the fairy couple, and the double crescent of the moon—signs of psychic and spiritual powers), he can wisely connect heart and brain.

20 January – 18 February

A Time of Lessons Learned

Five Swords

1st decan of Aquarius (20 – 29 January)

Do not belittle your problems, fears, and deficiencies. Work with them. Do not be afraid of them, quite to the contrary!

The times when you felt small and unimportant are behind you. You've come a long way. Looking back you are able to grasp earlier difficulties, fears, and uncertainties—and to let them go. Don't disconnect as soon as you face problems, but harness your full mental forces. Get help and assist others. In this way you will get rid of your feelings of helplessness and create a fresh feeling of well-being.

Don't throw in the towel. Don't let others berate you. Be prepared for criticism, and be your own best critic. You will discover new aspects as well as more sympathy.

"A River Runs Through It:" you suddenly grasp how the different strands of your life are all connected, you see the central theme. Discover the *meaning* of victories as well as of losses and respect the importance of experiences which express themselves in this way. Your happiness will grow when love and understanding grow.

Advice ➤ *There will be new success: you reach for the swords and come forward, even if your idea isn't yet ripe or perfect. This is fine. Just keep in mind how much of the power of superiors, law enforcement personal, or spiritual leaders depends less on the authority they have gained, but on our far too large patience, our frivolous powerlessness! Some sane audaciousness will save you from belittling yourself in case of an injustice.*

20 – 29 January

A Time of New Horizons

2ⁿᵈ decan of Aquarius (30 January – 8 February)

Six Swords

Y ou have started a journey, you are accompanied by others. The Six Swords can either be a burden or a meaningful piece of equipment—just as the persons in the image support each other, they drive and rest in turns, but can also become fixed to certain roles. Will the ferryman set out to reach new shores, or is he only a restless commuter between different worlds?

Clarify interests and needs. Let your own intelligence play the part of the punt pole of the image: a help on which you can lean and by which you can support yourself because it gives you *ground* contact. Never forget where you came from, and where you want to go to.

Old and new experiences mix. "i am/ growing along/ walls/ the bricks/ i have/ smashed/ but/ still i carry/ their pattern with me/ for a long time" *(H.C. Flemming)*.

Don't project onto others—respect the desistance, the differences, and the translation that is necessary to bring ideas across. Understand what your fellow humans need and explain to them what motivates you. Use all your ability to combine and mediate in order to let it flow between you and your fellow men—and in order for you to steer your own course in the current of events.

Discover the *experiences* and the motives *behind* the doctrines. Understand the *grounds* of what others basically do or say.

Get free from repetitive compulsions. Set out to reach new shores! ≺ *Advice*

30 January – 8 February

A Time of Personal Enigmas

Seven Swords

3rd decan of Aquarius (9 – 18 February)

M oving forward while looking back? Aimlessness or conscious retrospective?

Each person gives birth to a new truth in this world, and so each of us faces mysteries and riddles that exist only for us to find their solutions. This is our predetermined goal.

You have made your decision and in that way cleared the path. This indicates quite an amount of courage, but most of all the appreciative insight that it is you who can help yourself best—it simply is the easiest and most effective way! Stress each step. This card only indicates deceit, intrigue, vainness, or other unwanted meanings when you are not able to understand others—and/or even yourself.

Do not be frightened by problems and adversaries. Go your own way. Work with your dreams and really find your aims in love. This is true as well for all intellectual quests.

You take what you need; what you don't need you leave as it is; and you go your own way. You have understood that the many troubles and fights you have had to face were only because you had too little courage to follow your dreams, and that your courage decreased in the measure of waiting because you were too afraid to proceed or make the first step. The most important battles take place within you.

Advice ➤ *You face many fights and many difficulties only as long as you do not completely trust your own truth and mission in life. Understand all current controversies as a way to define your place. In this way, you will experience—and cause—important things.*

Processing of the suppressed and forgotten

The Pisces Month (19 February – 20 March)

The last month of the yearly cycle is often called the "waste paper basket." We again have to face whatever has been forgotten and suppressed in the course of the yearly cycle. We need to process things far more consciously now: either deal with them or let them go. Not only in the Christian tradition is this period a time of Lent. Even if you are not following a religion, fasting, meditation, and dealing with practical tasks can help you to process psychic residue and all things that have not yet been solved.

XVIII-The Moon

Everything here comes to the surface: even Cancer, the crawfish, which usually lives in dark, inaccessible places, comes up to the surface. And the Pearly Gates stand wide open and are clearly visible. In this sign, we may have to face and solve large emotions. Sometimes, you feel as if you are "dissolved" by this (no human figure in the picture!). Don't be daunted and refrain from howling at the moon. Take your time to clear

19 February – 20 March

155

Great emotions, dreams,
a new beginning soon

THE MOON

XII

THE HANGED MAN

Heaven, reversing
of ways

Love and search,
"savior"

KNIGHT of CUPS

all that which needs to be cleared and be prepared for an untroubled new beginning in the approaching spring.

XII-The Hanged Man

Pisces is defined by "I believe." Naturally enough, its element is Water. The "Hanged Man" has a clearly defined point of view: not earth, but heaven! His reality is heaven, that is religious belief, but also human convictions such as "Man must do whatever makes him happy." In times where you just do not know what to believe anymore, this card signifies that you need to turn everything upside down, that you need to test everything to the core. The card also tells you to get rid of unwanted addictions and dependencies!

Knight of Cups

Set off toward all you love. In case your cup is empty, return to the source and fill it again. When it is full, go out into the world and bring it to all others.

19 February – 20 March

A Time of Proofing and Trusting

ℋ

1ˢᵗ decan of Pisces
(19 – 28 or 29 February)

Eight Cups

Eight Cups represent an abundance of real, lived life, of a multitude of experience and results gained. And yet you need to move on now. Standing still would put you in danger even that which you have already achieved. We are talking about emotions which are so enormous that we can no longer hold them in individual cups; feelings that drag and carry us.

It is true that any path into the unknown is often enough dark and frightening. But this signals neither darkness nor loneliness. Day and night have their own special clarity, and there is a light that never goes out.

It is not easy to give up familiar ground. But possibly it is just the perfect time now to move away from achievements and habits which sustain a livelihood, but give no real fun. A new beginning can make you experience a passion for being in constant movement, and can make you feel the vitality in you and all around you.

Get rid of emotional half-truths. Everything flows. There is no other safety in your life than following the path you are on, and to follow the light of the sun as well as the gentle, yet determining impulses of the moon. You will feel snug and secure in the world.

Hopes and fears lead you toward the origin of your longing.

The red figure in the image follows the river (the inner down-grade) ◁ *Advice*
and, at the same time, moves uphill, into the mountains. We overcome obstacles and reach new heights when we just go with the flow, and make our inner flow the guideline for what we do.

19 – 28 or 29 February

A Time of Great Emotions

Nine Cups

2nd decan of Pisces
(1 – 10 March)

I t is a great joy when all waters flow freely. We are often afraid of our feelings. And yet we cannot live against our feelings for any period of time—they will get us in the end. And what do the cups contain? It is generally said that one should trust one's gut feelings. And yet there are untrue feelings or false intuitions! You have to differentiate between what makes sense and what does not. This may be difficult for the figure in the image. The Cups are far *behind* his back. Only in consciously looking for those who have been left behind, a *retrospective* as a form of *respect* for the needs of the soul of all concerned, will you make progress in your current questions.

Have the courage to make a difference! Don't be shocked by embarrassments or be fascinated by oddities. Stay true to your heart and sometimes "march to a different drummer"! You will gain the richness of great emotions without any unwanted side effects.

You accept your own deficiencies and merits. You are a darling of fortune: satisfaction, pleasure, quietness and harmony spring from your active participation in life and from your experiences. You trust yourself. "All of you is worth something if you will only own it" *(Sheldon B. Kopp).*

Advice ➤ **There is power in quietness. Live your emotions to the full – you will consider nothing human alien to you, and none of your most important needs will be left empty-handed! Play the complete repertoire of feelings and needs! Without continually assessing and judging you will be able to show your versatility and achieve successes that are really satisfying.**

1 – 10 March

A Time of Passions

3rd decan of Pisces
(11 – 21 March)

Ten Cups

Y ou live with great passions. They raise and fill your life.

But beware of fanciful pipe dreams and illusions! The Ten Cups in the rainbow may—at the most negative—represent a delusion, a passion which causes pain.

In a positive sense this card actually signifies really wonderful adventures and events. The rainbow is a symbol of God's commitment to the human race, a bridge between heaven and earth. It also represents the lucky union of earth and water (sun and rain). With this, it is a metaphor for creativity, for the fruitful merging of (human or personal) opposites of any kind!

With an open heart you will be able to absorb and emit great amounts of energy. You are like a force field in which you and others feel well. It is an art to trust yourself and each other, even marrying to venture into a shared design of living.

You will experience happiness which comes like a present, but which is only the final result of your willingness to be open, and to receive. "To see a world in a grain of sand, / And a heaven in a wild flower, / Hold infinity in the palm of your hand, / And eternity in an hour" *(William Blake).*

What you wish for will be realized by a colorful and multi-faceted life. You will find loves and relationships which completely fill you. Understand what others say – and what it actually means. Your readiness to work creatively with relationships and situations will fulfill your longings and desires. ≺ Advice

11 – 21 March

159

Lists of references

Illustration credits

❚ Cover: Maya prophecy © frenta – Fotolia.com ❚ p. 10 + 59: Sun stone © j.o.photodesign – Fotolia.com ❚ p. 24: storm © olly – Fotolia.com ❚ p. 27: *The Tower*, Tarot de Marseille, and *The Tower*, Aleister Crowley Thoth Tarot ❚ p. 33: *The Tower*, and *Judgment*, Tarot de Marseille ❚ p. 37: *The Star*, Visconti-Sforza Tarot ❚ p. 39: *Judgment*, Tarot de Marseille ❚ p. 46: gray-haired, attractive woman enjoying sunny fall © Danel – Fotolia.com ❚ p. 100: two butterflies on flowers © artjazz – Fotolia.com ❚ p. 105: Old bridge in misty autumn park © Gorilla – Fotolia.com ❚ p. 110: beautiful pink peony © sarsmis – Fotolia.com ❚ p. 115: River through woods © Elenathewise – Fotolia.com ❚ p. 120: Marguerite–land 3 © Patrizia Tilly – Fotolia.com ❚ p. 125: grapes 2 © ThKatz – Fotolia.com ❚ p. 130: sky © Sergey Tokarev – Fotolia.com ❚ p. 135: heartsickness © travelguide – Fotolia.com ❚ p. 140: Christmas Gift © Subbotina Anna – Fotolia.com ❚ p. 145: Matterhorn in winter © nickichen – Fotolia.com ❚ p. 150: winter © Leonid Tit – Fotolia.com ❚ p. 155: Alien Landscape © rolffimages – Fotolia.com ❚

Books by Rachel Pollack

78 Degrees of Wisdom. Aquarian Press/Thorsons, 1980, 1983, revised edition 1997
Tarot Wisdom. Llewellyn, 2008
The Forest of Souls. Llewellyn, 2003
The Shining Tribe Tarot (art and text). Llewellyn, 2001
Godmother Night (fiction, winner of the World Fantasy Award). St. Martin's, 1996

English language books by Johannes Fiebig

Tarot. Basics Waite: More than 800 pictures (with Evelin Burger). Llewellyn, 2012
Dali Tarot. Konigsfurt, 2004
The Complete Book of Tarot Spreads. (with Evelin Burger). Sterling, 1997